CENTRAL WINCHESTER

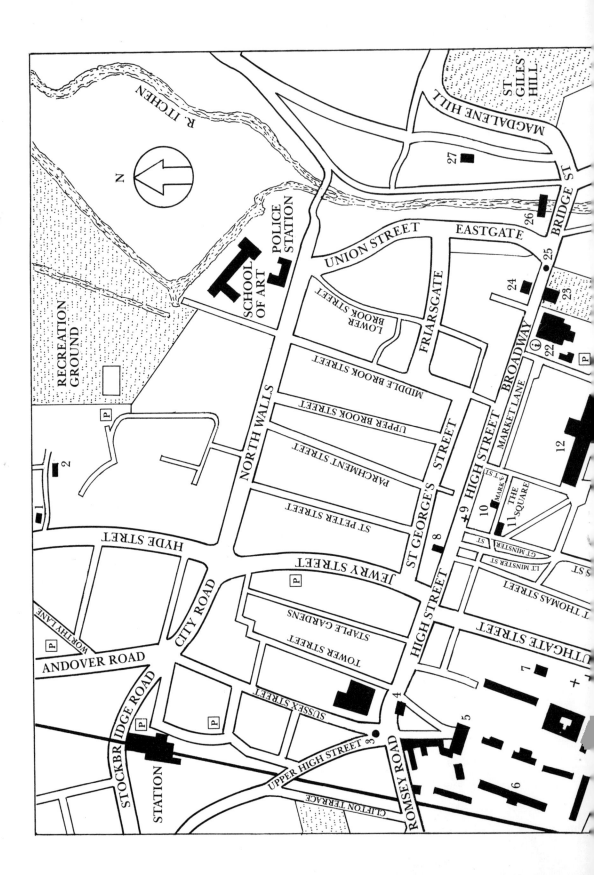

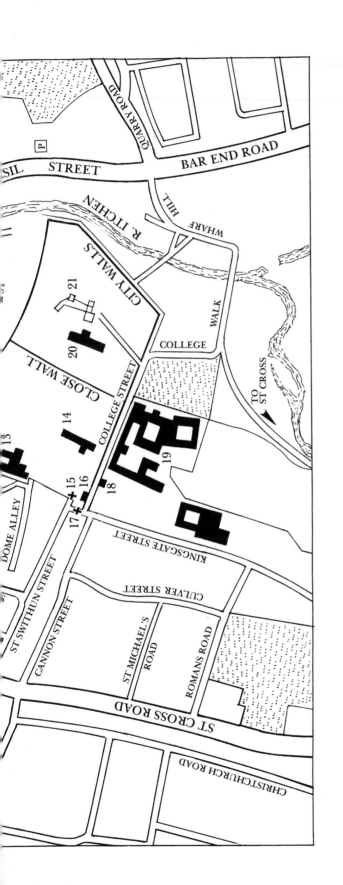

KEY

1 St Bartholomew, Hyde
2 Hyde Abbey Gateway
3 Obelisk
4 Westgate and Museum
5 Great Hall
6 Green Jackets Museum
7 Serle's House
8 God Begot House
9 Butter Cross
10 Eclipse Inn
11 City Museum
12 Cathedral
13 Deanery
14 Pilgrims' School
15 St Swithun's Gate
16 Cheyney House
17 Kingsgate
18 Jane Austen's House
19 Winchester College
20 Wolvesey Palace
21 Wolvesey Castle
22 Guildhall
23 Abbey House
24 St John's Hospital
25 King Alfred Statue
26 City Mill
27 St John the Baptist
P Parking
ⓘ Tourist information

0   ⅛   ¼ MILES
0   0.2   0.4 KILOMETRES

WINCHESTER

WINCHESTER

Text by
COLIN BADCOCK

With photographs by
ERNEST FRANKL

THE PEVENSEY PRESS
Cambridge England

Published by The Pevensey Press
6 De Freville Avenue, Cambridge CB4 1HR, UK

Acknowledgements
Photographs: Ernest Frankl, except 5: the author. Permission to
reproduce the following photographs is gratefully acknowledged:
4, 5, 21–34, by courtesy of the Dean and Chapter of Winchester
Cathedral; **5, 37–41, back cover,** by courtesy of the Warden and
Scholars of Winchester College.

Pp. 73-80 are based on material kindly provided by
Mr M. D. Kenney.

Maps: Carmen Frankl

Edited by Ruth Smith

Designed by Ruth Smith and Peter Dolton

Design and production in association with
Book Production Consultants, Cambridge

© Ernest Frankl and The Pevensey Press, 1988
First published 1988

ISBN 0 907115 52 7 paperback only

Origination by Anglia Graphics
Typesetting in Baskerville by Witwell Ltd, Southport
Printed and bound in Portugal
by Printer Portuguesa Grafica, Lda

Front cover The brothers' quarters of the medieval almshouse of
St Cross, on the south-eastern side of the city.

Frontispiece A view along the Cathedral's south aisle from the
west, showing the rounded Norman architecture of the transept
beyond the aisle's Gothic pointed arches.

Back cover A medieval misericord carving under one of the seats
of the choir stalls in Winchester College Chapel.

Contents

History

W inchester, now a quiet cathedral city and country town, was once the capital of England and the seat of a bishop whose diocese spread from Southwark – just outside London – to the Isle of Wight and the Channel Islands.

The Saxon kings of Wessex made Winchester their capital, and when William the Conqueror landed he knew he had to capture the city – England's administrative centre – to secure control of the kingdom. But he also realised the strategic and commercial advantages of London (as the Romans had done earlier), and it gradually became the seat of government. Winchester's greatest days were over by the end of the 13th century. Nevertheless, up to the time of Charles II kings of Britain were conscious that Winchester gave better witness to the antiquity of their throne than London could, and chose it as the scene of major royal events. Edward the Confessor had been crowned here; and here Henry VIII entertained the Emperor Charles V, and Mary Tudor married Philip of Spain.

The huge diocese of Winchester was founded in the 7th century when Hedda, bishop of Wessex, moved his episcopal seat here from Dorchester-on-Thames. Winchester's bishops provided ten Chancellors of England as well as two Cardinals and two Papal Legates. In 1569 the Channel Islands were added to their already enormous territory, which remained intact until 1905. Then the diocese of Southwark was formed, and in 1927 those of Guildford and Portsmouth. But the bishop of Winchester remains one of the five senior bishops of the land, with the exalted office (since 1348) of Prelate of the Order of the Garter.

The tide of national events receded from Winchester in the late Middle Ages, and the 16th-century Reformation eclipsed the Church's all-pervading power; but there have been no sweeping developments in more recent times to obliterate the evidence of the past, and many reminders of the great periods of early English history give Winchester its present-day charm and character.

1 Hamo Thornycroft's statue (1901) of Alfred the Great (849–900) in the Broadway. King of the West Saxons, Alfred drove the Vikings out of southern England and later became overlord of all England; he is regarded as the founder of the unified nation. A scholar and a dedicated Christian as well as a great military leader, he found time between campaigns to translate Boethius' Consolation of Philosophy, *Bede's* History *and Gregory the Great's* Pastoral Care.

Ancient Britons

To find the homes of the earliest settlers of ancient Britain, we need to look for landscape that was neither forest nor swamp. Salisbury Plain is an obvious example, and so are the chalklands of central Hampshire. The River Itchen is easily crossable as it runs from water meadows north of Winchester between two chalk hills, St Giles' to the east and St Paul's to the west (the present High Street runs from one to the other). Here lay a Celtic settlement before Romans or Anglo-Saxons were on the scene. Earthworks and relics testify to the existence of Caer Gwent, the White City of the Celts, most notably the iron age hill-fort and earthworks of **St Catherine's Hill (2)**

7

just beyond the present by-pass. Here in about 400 BC a Celtic chieftain turned the hill into a typical iron age fortress, with a stockade at the top and a trench cut round the belly of the hill.

When the Belgae came to these parts in about 150 BC and chose Winchester for their market town they sacked the Celtic fort. But they never occupied the hill themselves; nor did the Romans when they arrived in the 50s AD, though no doubt they took their best girls up the hill for a picnic – some of them left their brooches behind.

St Catherine's Hill is one of Winchester's best-known landmarks. It takes its name from a saint whose cult became popular in England in Norman times, and who was said to have been a virgin queen of Alexandria in the 4th century AD. She was condemned to be broken on the wheel by the Emperor Maxentius, and her body was miraculously transferred to the top of Mount Sinai. So it became common in the 11th century to crown hilltops with chapels to St Catherine; there are three such in Hampshire, and here beneath the clump of trees on the crest of the hill are the foundations of a chapel. (They were carefully excavated in 1926, and covered up again.)

In Saxon times St Catherine's Hill was part of a large gift of land from King Cynegils to the Church of Wessex. It remained church property until 1930, when the Old Wykehamist Lodge of Freemasons purchased it from the Ecclesiastical Commissioners and presented it to Winchester College. (Students of the College are called Wykehamists after the founder, William of Wykeham.) What are now the College playing fields were formerly either farm land or marsh, and for four centuries the top of 'Hills' was the only recreation ground for Wykehamists. Thither they trooped twice a week in crocodile to indulge in games, badger-baiting or football, or to tread the ancient turf-cut labyrinth or 'miz-maze', which you can still do today. Then the Prefect of Hall cried 'Domum' ('homeward') and they all trooped back again.

Twice a year, in memory of those old days, the six hundred members of the school walk to the top of St Catherine's Hill in the early morning, listen to a psalm and a prayer, and walk back to their houses for breakfast.

The Romans

The story of Roman Winchester has to be pieced together from a few coins, portions of mosaic pavement found in the town centre, three inscriptions mostly of letters rather than words, and a good deal of intelligent conjecture. The Romans seem to have reached the Belgic town soon after the Emperor Claudius' invasion of Britain in 43 AD, and gave it the name of Venta Belgarum, Market-place of the Belgae. They built a walled city; parts of the existing medieval walls are Roman in origin. From gates at the four points of the compass Roman roads radiated to settlements such as Silchester, Southampton and Salisbury.

The present High Street was probably the *decumanus* (main street) of the Roman town, with a grid of streets – which partly survives – running off it. Of the major buildings which must have existed, no trace remains.

Even less can be said of how the Romans left in the 5th century. There is no hint of struggle or catastrophe, and presumably the mixed race of Roman bureaucracy withdrew, like the soldiery, to the remnants of the

2 *St Catherine's Hill,
an enduring aspect of
the Winchester scene:
it was inhabited
during the iron age,
long before
Winchester existed (c.
400–150 BC), when
Celtic tribes settled
here. The River
Itchen, seen in the
foreground, rises
among the watercress
beds of Alresford (to
the east) and flows
south to join the sea
at Southampton.*

Roman Empire on the continent, or merged with the tribes arriving from northern Europe.

After the Romans – King Arthur?

The departure of the Romans was followed by the resistance of the Romano-Celtic Britons to those invaders from the continent whom history calls Angles, Saxons and Jutes. Legend makes King Arthur and his knights the heroes of this struggle. Though we may take 'Arthur' as an historical person who perhaps learned his military skills from the Romans and used them against the invading Saxons, we should be more cautious about the title 'king', and reject altogether the idea of him ruling lands overseas. We must content ourselves with the concept of a great warrior living in the chaotic 6th century. Around his deeds grew a great web of myths and fairy tales (some call him the 'heir of the fairy king Oberon'), repeated and exaggerated for two dark centuries until first recorded by the chroniclers Nennius (in the 8th century) and Geoffrey of Monmouth (in the 12th).

Some romantics, but few scholars, see the chalky White City of Winchester as Arthur's Camelot, and the legend has decent antiquity. At the top of the High Street in the Great Hall built by Henry III in the 1220s you can still see the 'Round Table of King Arthur' (**3**). This great circle of wood

was first mentioned in writing in the 15th century, and is in fact older than that. It was repainted under Henry VIII, who in 1522 proudly showed the Tudor rose in the middle of it to the Hapsburg Charles V as proof of the antiquity of his throne. The table does not, of course, prove anything of the kind, but it does indicate that the legend that links King Arthur with Winchester is four or five centuries old.

The Saxons

The greatness of Winchester as a capital city and centre of learning and religious foundations starts with the Saxons – the 'New English' as opposed to the 'Ancient Britons'; and the period of the Saxon greatness of Winchester runs through the four centuries from the mid 600s to the Norman Conquest of 1066. Wintanceaster (the Saxon form of the city's modern name, of which the 13th-century abbreviation 'Winton' is still sometimes used) was the capital of the Saxon kings of Wessex: the bones of six Saxon kings and two Saxon bishops rest to this day in reliquary chests in the Cathedral (4). The story centres round four persons – two kings and two sainted bishops.

The first of these is Cynegils, King of Wessex. His conversion to Christianity by St Birinus in 635 began Winchester's life as a religious centre and a royal town, the seat of a king and the see of a bishop. It led to the construction, probably in the reign of his son, of a grand church of cathedral proportions, Oldminster. This lay just north of the present Norman Cathedral which replaced it; its foundations, excavated in modern times, have been clearly marked in the grass and an explanatory notice-board stands close to the west doors of the Cathedral. To this centre of worship Hedda, bishop of Wessex since 676, moved his throne from Dorchester-on-Thames, to become the first bishop of Winchester. There were to be 35 Saxon bishops here before the Normans came.

The next figure, the saintly Swithun, is more shadowy. He became bishop of Winchester in 852, and was the confidant of the Saxon kings Egbert and Ethelwulf – a crucial role at a time when the Danish invasions were at their height and threatening the very walls of Winchester. Exactly what St Swithun did, either by organising fortifications or by rallying the spirits of Hampshiremen, is not clear, but he was greatly revered both in life and after his death. Pilgrimages to his shrine began in Saxon times, and continued increasingly until the Reformation put a stop to such veneration. His bones were laid to rest outside Oldminster, moved inside in about 980 as his cult grew, and moved again to the new Norman Cathedral in 1093. Here the shrine of St Swithun became a centre of pilgrimage second only to that of St Thomas of Canterbury. Legend has it that when St Swithun's bones were moved from their Saxon resting place his spirit wept and rain began which continued for 40 days; hence the popular·lore that if it rains on St Swithun's Day (15 July) it will rain for the next 40 days.

Greatest of all the Saxon figures is King Alfred. As king of Wessex he was the only successful opponent of the Danes, finally defeating them at Ethandune, near Chippenham, and by the Treaty of Wedmore (878) securing their retreat north-east of the line from London to Chester. Wessex was left to peace and orderly civilisation. Under Alfred Winchester grew as a centre of religion and learning and civilised arts emanating from monastic foundations under royal patronage. Two new religious houses arose – Newminster to the west of the existing Cathedral, and Nunnaminster (a nunnery) between the present Broadway and Colebrook Street. Alfred died (900) when Newminster was hardly begun, and was buried originally in Oldminster, to be reinterred in Newminster beside the high altar. The two foundations were built so close together that worshippers in one could hear the offices being chanted in the other, and in 1110 Newminster was moved to Hyde Mead, north of the town, changing its name to Hyde Abbey. Hyde Abbey Gateway (in King Alfred Place off Hyde Street) marks where it stood. The Newminster buildings became part of the Cathedral complex. Alfred's remains were transferred yet again, in solemn procession; but Hyde Abbey was pulled down during the Reformation, in 1787 the site was chosen for a new county gaol, and now there is no trace of the burial place of the greatest of the Saxon kings. A thousand years after Alfred's death the statue of him by Hamo Thornycroft was erected in the Broadway at the bottom of the High Street (1).

St Ethelwold is the last of our four great Saxons. Born in Winchester, he served under St Dunstan in Glastonbury, and was with him one of the major reforming influences on the 10th-century church in England, in touch with continental monasticism. He became bishop of Winchester in 963 and drew up the *Regularis Concordia*, which brought order and Benedictine discipline to monastic life. Under him there was a new flowering of scholarly and literary work in the religious houses, and he particularly fostered the art of manuscript illumination, in what became known as the Winchester style. In his time Newminster was reformed; Oldminster was reconstructed to house the shrine of St Swithun, and later it received the shrine of St Ethelwold himself.

The scene in Saxon Winchester was dominated by powerful monuments of church and state. In what must have been a rather cluttered area to the south of the High Street (roughly from the Broadway to St Thomas Street) lay an enclosure containing Newminster, Oldminster and Nunnaminster with their attendant monastic buildings. There must have been a royal residence for the Saxon kings, perhaps to the west of Newminster, but still south of the High Street. By Alfred's time there was a mint to manufacture coins of the realm, and no doubt other administrative buildings. To the north of the High Street ran a straggle of humbler houses, while to the east was the Saxon bishop's residence at Wolvesey, and the whole was enclosed by a city wall.

The high-water mark of Winchester as a royal seat and capital city was reached when Edward the Confessor, the last of the Saxon kings, was crowned in Oldminster on Easter Day 1043, and received gifts and embassies from abroad. After him came William the Conqueror, and with the Normans the centre of things began to move to London.

The Norman Conquest

To conquer England in 1066 it was vital to secure Winchester. When the Normans accepted the surrender of the citizens in November 1066, they were not total strangers to the city, nor was Winchester unused to strangers from the continent. Edward the Confessor's mother was Emma of Normandy, and her second husband was Canute the Dane (king of England 1016–35). Emma's bones and Canute's lie among those of the Saxon kings and bishops in the Cathedral. Queen Edith, widow of Edward the Confessor and sister of the last pre-Conquest king, Harold, lived on peacefully in Winchester after it had become the seat of a Norman king and a Norman bishop. The Conqueror built his palace in the area of the present St Lawrence's Church, and established his treasury and royal mint in the city (nothing of these remains).

In 1070 the first Norman bishop replaced his Saxon predecessor Stigand. This was Walkelin, a kinsman of King William, and it was he who

4 *One of the six mortuary chests on the presbytery screens in the Cathedral. Four date from 1525, the other two are copies made in 1661 after damage by soldiers in the Commonwealth era. They contain bones of kings and bishops from the 7th century to the 11th: King Cynegils (611–43), King Cenwalh (643–72), King Egbert (802–39), King Ethelwulf (839–58) and King Canute (1016–35) and his queen Emma; and Bishops Wine (662–3), Elfwine (1032–4) and Stigand (1047–70). The pelican and mitre below are emblems of Bishop Fox (bishop of Winchester 1501–28), who caused the screens and chests to be erected.*

undertook the construction of a cathedral in the grand Norman style. In the spring of 1079 building began. Down came Oldminster, in came stone from the Isle of Wight and timber from the royal forest near Alresford, and on 8 April 1093 the new building, partly overlapping the foundations of Oldminster, was dedicated for worship 'with the utmost exultation and rejoicing'. Slowly new monastic buildings grew up to the south, and the work of the Benedictine order was transferred from Oldminster. The

Norman parts of the Cathedral (5) can still be seen in the tower, transepts and crypt – though the tower is the second Norman attempt, for the wicked King William Rufus was buried under the first one in 1100, and seven years later it collapsed in protest and had to be rebuilt.

Rufus' brother Henry I died in 1135 leaving no living son, and Winchester was at the eye of the succession storm. Henry de Blois, bishop of Winchester and grandson of the Conqueror, backed the claim to the throne of his brother Stephen against their cousin Matilda. The bishop's castle at Wolvesey became a fortified stronghold, the royal palace was burnt, chaos reigned and according to the Anglo-Saxon Chronicle for 1137 'men said openly that Christ slept, and his saints'.

The Middle Ages

Henry II of Anjou (1154–89), Matilda's son, restored peace and order. Thomas à Becket was consecrated archbishop of Canterbury in Winchester Cathedral by Henry de Blois in 1162, and his martyrdom by the king's knights gave rise to a pilgrimage shrine at Canterbury that was to eclipse St Swithun's in Winchester. But Winchester and its wool trade flourished, enjoying the privileges of 18 royal charters granted between 1155 and 1561.

The great Benedictine foundation of the Cathedral, proprietor of manors stretching across southern England, had a full range of monastic buildings

5 *The Cathedral from the roof of Winchester College Chapel, with the College's Middle Gate and Outer Gate in the foreground: a view that emphasises the great extent of the nave (which extended 40 feet further west in Norman times) and the transition in styles from the Norman tower and transept to the early-13th-century east end.*

covering most of the present Cathedral Close. In the scriptorium the fine work of the Winchester manuscript school, with traditions going back to the time of Alfred, reached its peak during the bishopric of Henry de Blois (1129-73). One of its masterpieces, the splendidly illuminated Winchester Bible, can be seen in the Cathedral Library.

In the 14th century a new disaster struck. The Black Death reached Winchester in 1348, to return in 1361, 1369 and 1379. According to some accounts threequarters of the population died in the first year of the plague. It was the start of a steady decline in the fortunes of the city.

Nevertheless, out of evil some good was to come, and, as so often, troubled times produced a man to match the moment. William of Wykeham had become both bishop of Winchester and Chancellor of England in 1367, and he set himself to replenish the diminished ranks of the clerkly, literate, administrative class. From his own resources, which were considerable, he first founded New College in Oxford (1379), and then in 1382 received from Richard II a royal charter to found Winchester College (**5, 37-41**), which has some claim to be the oldest school in England in continuous operation in its original buildings. It is interesting to reflect that this school, which has lasted for six hundred years, received its charter only five years after Wycliffe began his attack on bishops and the Church, three years after the last visitation of the Black Death, and a bare year after the Peasants' Revolt. Not many people can have seen those days as an apt moment to start building for the next six centuries.

Wykeham's predecessor, Bishop Edington, had begun the transformation of the Cathedral nave from rough Norman work to the new Perpendicular style. Leaving Edington's two westernmost bays, Wykeham converted the rest of the nave to its present soaring elegance. (Those who regret the loss of the Norman nave and the totality of a Norman building may be comforted that what was lost was not perhaps of the best Norman workmanship.)

The great building, with the longest nave in Europe (**22**) - once even longer than it is now - continued as a Benedictine monastic house up to the Reformation, and continued its royal connections well beyond. Here Henry III was baptised in 1207, and Prince Arthur, elder brother of Henry VIII, in 1486; here King John was received back into Mother Church in 1213, and Henry IV was married in 1403. Here also, at immense expense, Mary Tudor was married to Philip II of Spain on 25 July 1554. And in 1979 Queen Elizabeth II and Prince Philip came to the Maundy Day service which marked the Cathedral's nine hundredth anniversary.

The Reformation

Reforms can be uncomfortable, and for most of England's religious houses the Reformation was extremely so. Reform was certainly needed, and was already beginning in Winchester under the good Bishop Fox. There would probably have been a general reformation of the Church even without Henry VIII's need for a divorce, which led to the break with Rome. But the Dissolution of the monasteries (1538) - and of all enclosed religious houses - altered the face of Winchester. First Hyde Abbey (to which the Saxon Newminster had been moved in 1110) was destroyed. Next the great nunnery of St Mary's Abbey, founded by King Alfred as Nunnaminster, was disbanded and razed in spite of the vigour of its last abbess, leaving desolate a large area of the city between Colebrook Street and Wolvesey. On the other hand Winchester College survived, indeed it benefited by the destruction of St Elizabeth's College, a chantry for lay priests in the meadow by College Walk, and by the dissolution of a Carmelite friary off Kingsgate Street, for it acquired their land.

The fate of the great Benedictine Cathedral Church and Priory might have been worse, but for an early example of the English gift for muddling through periods of high crisis. What had been a monastery with a prior and monks became a cathedral with a dean and chapter. William Kingsmill, the last prior, became the first dean, and his monks filled the new chapter. There were losses, certainly, but some treasure remained, and the decay of the monastic buildings that once filled the Close owes more to the neglect of a later bishop than to the Reformation itself. In 1541 royal documents were issued to establish the new dean and chapter, and a coat of arms granted to the new body.

Nevertheless, one great blow fell. Dark deeds are best done in the dark, and at 3 a.m. on Saturday 21 September 1538 three royal commissioners stole into the Cathedral, wrecked the ancient shrine of St Swithun and the high altar, and stole silver to the amount of 2000 marks. Their names were Thomas Wriothesley, Richard Pollard and John Williams. We still have the report they wrote to Thomas Cromwell, the king's right-hand man, boasting of their intention to 'sweep away all the rotten bones that be called relics'. Thus the remains of St Swithun, like those of King Alfred, were lost for ever.

The Civil War and After

The Civil War was the last of the great disasters to come to Winchester and, with the exception of the Black Death, probably the worst. Within Winchester loyalties were divided between King Charles I and Oliver Cromwell. The royal castle by the Westgate was in private hands in 1642 when war started and the owner was a Parliamentarian, but the royalist cause revived until Cromwell himself directed his cannons on the city in September 1645. The division of loyalties was well illustrated in 1648, when Charles I, a prisoner on his way to London, arrived at the Westgate. The loyalist Mayor of Winchester received him with all proper courtesy due to a sovereign, only to be set upon by the Cromwellian guards.

After the execution of the king in 1649, Winchester suffered far more from the Puritan Commonwealth government than it had ever endured from the Reformation of Henry VIII. Winchester College again was lucky, but few other institutions escaped unharmed. The royal castle at the top of the High Street and the bishop's castle at Wolvesey (43) were destroyed, the dean and chapter were abolished, and the Cathedral itself only just avoided destruction. Commonwealth soldiers entered the building, wrecking the west window, damaging the choir stalls, breaking statues, and looking with a hostile eye at the chantries. A little damage was done to William of Wykeham's chantry, but it was saved from a worse fate – so the story goes – by the intervention of the Commonwealth officer, Nathaniel Fiennes, who was himself a Wykehamist.

6 *The medieval porch and chapel of St John's Hospital in the Broadway, one of the earliest of the city's many charitable foundations and now over seven hundred years old. In medieval times this was the starting point of the city's most important procession, on Corpus Christi Day, and here each autumn the Mayor was elected.*

It seemed that nothing would ever be the same again in England, but after the restoration of King Charles II in 1660 normality returned to Winchester. There was a moment when it might again have become a royal city, for Charles started to build a palace here, designed by Wren, to show respect for the ancient capital and to point to the antiquity of his restored throne. The palace was to be on the site of the Norman castle, and would have looked downhill through an avenue of trees to the west front of the Cathedral. However the original grand design and attendant landscaping were never completed, and Wren's little-admired building was destroyed by fire in 1894. In the early years of the 18th century Queen Anne likewise cultivated royal connections with Winchester: she intended to turn Wren's King's House into a residence for her consort, Prince George of Denmark. In vain; death intervened and the grandeur and the courtiers failed to return. But the charm and taste of the 17th- and 18th-century houses of the ordinary gentry adorn Winchester to this day (**7–10**).

The Modern City

Winchester today is a county town whose shops and offices serve a wide area of Hampshire. Banks, building societies, estate agents, insurance companies and chain stores – and the offices of the Hampshire County Council (locally known as 'The Kremlin') – fill its streets. House prices soar

17

7–10 *Characteristic Winchester housefronts: above (left) 40 Little Minster Street; (right) Mason's Yard, St Thomas Street; below (left) 70 Kingsgate Street; (right) The Old Vine Inn, Great Minster Street.*

as more and more commuters move in, and take the 60-minute train journey to London for their daily bread. Large housing estates cluster round the ancient centre, at Stanmore and Badger Farm to the south, and at Winnall and Weeke to the north.

Since World War II light industry has moved in and the Army has moved out. At the beginning of the Napoleonic Wars in 1793, Wren's old King's House, begun as a palace for Charles II, proved its usefulness as a barracks to train and discipline troops ready to move to the continent. In 1858 the Rifle Depot was set up here as a base for those light infantry, fast moving rifle regiments, who had made their name in the Peninsular War. So the Rifle Brigade and the 60th Rifles, King's Royal Rifle Corps, made their home here, and the Barracks remained the depot after World War II of the Royal Green Jackets, an amalgamation of the Light Infantry regiments, until they moved in 1986 to their new barracks at Flowerdown, north of Winchester.

Meanwhile the Hampshire Regiment, formed in 1881 from units that had been raised in the county in the 18th century, and granted the title of The Royal Hampshire in 1946 after distinguished action in World War II, keeps its regimental museum at Serle's House, though its troops are now elsewhere; and the Royal Hussars have recently set up their museum on the Barracks site. All this area remains a monument to the days when Winchester was a considerable garrison town, but those days are now past.

The city still contains an ancient independent school at Winchester College, a new Sixth Form College inheriting the traditions of Peter

11 *A block of the Upper Barracks, occupied by the Royal Green Jackets until 1986. It was built in the early 1900s with its foundations resting on the walls of Wren's palace for Charles II.*

12 *The almshouses of Christ's Hospital, dating from 1607, were endowed in 1586 by Peter Symonds, a London cloth merchant, as a thank-offering to his native city.*

Symonds' 17th-century grammar school, a School of Art, and King Alfred's College, a College of Higher Education. These and the great Hospital of St Cross still flourish in modern Winchester, enjoying the benefactions of those who put money towards the care of the old and the nurture of the young – the twin marks of a civilised society, summed up by an inscription that adorns Christ's Hospital Almshouses in Symonds Street (**12**):

CHRIST'S HOSPITAL
Which was founded
In the Year of Our Lord 1607
By PETER SYMONDS
a Native of Winchester
and afterwards a Mercer
in the City of London.
The Endowments of this House
are applied to the maintenance
of Six Old Men, One Matron, and Four Boys;
and also to the assistance
of one Scholar
in each of the Two English Universities.
The Name of such a Benefactor
Is remembered with gratitude by Posterity.

A Visit to the City

From the Castle to the Cathedral

It is best to start at the **Castle**, at the top of the High Street beside the Westgate. Imagine the rectangle of walled Roman Winchester running east and west across a map, with the High Street running east and west across the middle of it. At the Westgate you are standing halfway up the left (west) side of that rectangle. There was a Westgate here in Roman times, and a Saxon gate when the Normans arrived in 1066. It is the highest point of the city proper.

Walk towards the Great Hall of the castle and look down on the recent excavations in front of it. You are looking at the remains of a round tower and three sally port passages, which formed the northern tip of a huge Norman castle which stretched southwards behind the Great Hall across the Barracks area as far as St James' Lane, in a walled and towered compound covering more than 4 acres. With this in mind you will not make the mistake of supposing that the Great Hall is all there was to the Norman castle: it is all that remains, a tiny part of the original ensemble.

In 1067 William the Conqueror ordered a castle to be built here, on St Paul's Hill, with the Roman city wall as its boundaries to south and west. It was a necessary part of his strategic plan for the conquest of the rest of Britain. Here he placed his treasury and exchequer, his officials and his soldiers. It was both a fortress and an administrative centre, but not yet a royal residence. His own palace was down in the centre of the town near the Cathedral.

Perhaps the most important thing in the Conqueror's castle was the treasury. When King William Rufus was killed while hunting in the New Forest, his younger brother Henry rode straight from the hunt to secure the treasury, and so the throne, before anyone could think of the claims of his eldest brother, Robert Duke of Normandy. As Henry I he began to use the castle as a residence.

By Henry II's time (1154–89) the function of the castle was changing. The Norman kings no longer used the royal palace near the Cathedral, and the administrative centre of the kingdom was moving to London. The 4-acre site ceased to be a fortress or seat of government, and began simply to be a place for the king and his court to live when in Winchester.

Modernisation of the castle was completed in the reign of Henry III (1216–72). Sometimes called Henry of Winchester, he was born and baptised in the city and spent 18 Christmasses here. He rebuilt the defences, made more comfortable living quarters and built the Great Hall, the surviving monument of his attachment to Winchester.

His son, Edward I (1272–1307), was too busy hammering the Scots to

13 *The Westgate's 13th-century side, facing the High Street. A city gate has stood here since Roman times. The upper room was formerly the local prison: inmates had no means of washing themselves or their clothes, and those who could not afford to pay the gaoler what he asked for food and drink depended on the charity of friends and relatives to keep them alive. 16th-century records list civic expenses for the gaol's savage administration: 1p for whipping vagabonds, 2½p for mending shackles and 12½p for chains for the prisoners.*

spend much time here, but on one of his occasional visits, at Easter in 1302, disaster struck: the royal apartments caught fire at night, and he and his queen were lucky to escape. After this, royalty never resided in the castle again. It ceased altogether to be royal when Elizabeth I handed it over to the city, and at the start of the Civil War in 1642 it belonged to a Parliamentarian citizen. Royalist troops reoccupied it but had to surrender in the face of Oliver Cromwell's cannons in 1645. During the Commonwealth the destruction of the royal castle was ordered, but the strength of the foundations and of Henry III's defences nearly caused the demolition squad to abandon the project as hopeless, and it was not completed; the **Great Hall** survives.

Built between 1222 and 1236, this room is a double cube, entered now by a Victorian doorway of 1845. Walk across the hall diagonally to your left and look through the door giving on to Queen Eleanor's Garden (restored in the style of a medieval garden, with old-fashioned roses, foxgloves, madonna lilies, honeysuckle and a vine-covered arbour, and reopened by the Queen Mother in July 1986). The castle once spread over all the area ahead of you, now covered by the Barracks buildings.

Besides serving as the hall of a royal castle, the Great Hall was the venue for Parliaments, held here by Edward III in 1330, by Richard II in 1393 and on more than 20 occasions up to 1449. These sessions are recalled on the east wall, decorated (in 1874) with the names of all the knights of the shire who represented Winchester at Parliament from 1283 to 1868. Courts of Law also sat in this room – from the itinerant justices of Henry III's day to the Assizes of the present century, which moved only in 1974 to the modern flint and stone law courts to the east of the castle. In 1603 Sir Walter Ralegh stood trial for treason in the Great Hall and was condemned. Now cleared of the clutter of docks and jury-boxes, the hall can be seen as it was in the Middle Ages, but a well-used grey judge's bench is preserved as a reminder of the law's long tenure.

The bronze statue of Queen Victoria, looking rather stranded in its corner, is the first full-scale public work of Alfred Gilbert (designer of Eros in London's Piccadilly Circus) – according to Rodin, 'the finest thing of its kind in modern times'. It was commissioned to mark the queen's Golden Jubilee (1887); Gilbert's mother modelled for the figure. The fantastic beaten metal crown – a reconstruction (1910) by Gilbert of the original, which shattered – and the crowd of allegorical figures round the throne are characteristically elaborate touches. The city council originally intended the statue for the hall, then decided to put it outside (hence Gilbert's use of bronze); for some years it stood in the Abbey Grounds, arriving here only in 1910.

'King Arthur's Round Table' (3), 18 feet across and weighing more than a ton, now hangs on the west wall of the Great Hall. Nobody quite knows how the connection arose between Winchester and the Romano-Celtic hero 'Arthur' of the 5th or 6th century AD. We do know that the Great Hall of Henry III was decorated by a wheel of fortune, and perhaps this round table is its replacement. But whatever the reason, the table has been in this hall at least since the 15th century, and probably longer than that.

Certainly it was originally a table, and had 12 legs supporting its rim, and one in the middle. The excellent booklet on Winchester Castle and the

14 Looking down the High Street through the Westgate. This side of the gate was renovated in the 14th century, when the city defences were strengthened in readiness for a feared French invasion.

Great Hall by Professor Biddle and Mrs Clayre tells us that modern dating methods (both study of the tree rings in the oak of which it is made, and radio-carbon dating) point to its construction between 1250 and 1280, most probably in the reign of Edward I, the last king to live in the castle. Their examination of the table also reveals that it was painted for the first time in about 1520, with a Tudor rose in the middle, the names of 24 knights of King Arthur round the edge, and the figure of King Arthur at the top – originally in the likeness of the youthful King Henry VIII, obscured now by a repainting in 1789. This was in preparation for a state visit: Henry showed the newly painted table to the Hapsburg Emperor Charles V to indicate the antiquity of his own throne. 'It was a neat point', says Professor Biddle, 'to make to a man who had recently become Holy Roman Emperor over Henry's own claims.'

From the Great Hall make for the 19th-century Westgate Hotel and go a few steps beyond it (with the brick County Council Offices of 1960 on your right) to the **Obelisk**. This monument (1754) commemorates the plague which struck Winchester in 1665 and again, more severely, in 1666 – a horror which had not occurred since the last visitation of the Black Death in 1379. Entire families were wiped out, the dead were buried communally

25

15 *Serle's House in Southgate Street, an 18th-century family house which is now the museum of the Royal Hampshire Regiment – a company formed in 1881 from two units first raised in the county in the 18th century. The title 'Royal' was earned during World War II in Europe and Africa with action which also won the regiment the freedom of the city.*

beyond St Catherine's Hill in Plague Pits Valley (still called 'Death Pits' by Wykehamists), and markets moved outside the afflicted city to the spot where the Obelisk now stands.

From the Obelisk you have an excellent view of the **Westgate** (13, 14; 12th–14th centuries), the medieval successor of the Roman gate which stood at this point of the Roman city wall. Of the five gates of the medieval city only this and Kingsgate (to the south of the centre) survive. It is a notable defensive work, with a machicolated parapet and two inverted key-hole apertures through which the earliest hand-held mortars could be fired. There was once a portcullis, and possibly a drawbridge. It is hard to believe that until 1959 all traffic entering and leaving the city at this point passed through the narrow arch of this gate.

The chamber above the gate, entered by a steep modern staircase on the south side, is now a small and attractive **museum**, containing 16th- and 17th-century armour, the graffiti of prisoners held here – from the 16th century to the 18th this room was a gaol for city debtors and malefactors – and an attractive wooden ceiling with part of its frieze, made and painted for the chamber of Warden White in Winchester College (probably for Queen Mary's visit in 1554), and restored and placed here in 1980.

The roof of the Westgate, easily reached, offers a good view of the full stretch of the **High Street**. It runs west to east (or, if you prefer, from Arthur to Alfred), from the high ground of St Paul's Hill across the valley bottom to the statue of King Alfred and the site of the Eastgate, where the ridge of St Giles' Hill rises beyond. Inevitably banks, building societies, estate agents and chain stores have replaced the family shops with their proprietors living above them which many residents still remember. Nevertheless individual façades of great charm and character remain. The ensemble of styles from all periods and the perspective of the slope combine to create the quintessential English high street.

As you walk downhill your eye is caught by Elisabeth Frink's *Horse and Rider* (1975), equestrian and at the same time slightly pedestrian, erected where formerly an ancient ilex arose from a deep bed of its own dropped leaves. At the corner of **Southgate Street**, further down to the right, runs the rather mean brick line of the Black Swan buildings. In 1932 these unworthily replaced the old Black Swan Hotel, where, it will be recalled, Sherlock Holmes and Dr Watson lunched while engaged on the Adventure of the Copper Beeches. Watson had consulted Bradshaw, and found that a train at half past nine was due at Winchester at 11.30, and would get them down in time to meet their worried client at the Black Swan at noon – 'an inn of repute in the High Street, at no distance from the station, and there we found the young lady waiting for us'.

In Southgate Street, just after the entrance (on the right) to the Royal Hussars Regimental Museum, you come to **Serle's House** (early 18th century), once the town house of a Catholic family, now remodelled as the musuem of the Royal Hampshire Regiment (**15**). Its ground, and the whole area behind it now occupied by the Peninsula Barracks buildings, were formerly filled by the Norman castle. Later Wren began building a palace here for Charles II (1683), but only one wing was completed when the king died in 1685, and now only the Corinthian columns of the King's House survive, adorning the façade (1900) of the Long Block of the Barracks, which were built after fire destroyed Wren's work in 1894. The energetic should continue down Southgate Street past a fine early Victorian terrace on the left (marred only by one modern office building in leprous brick), and return to the High Street via St Swithun and St Thomas Streets. St Swithun Street branches off at the site of the former Southgate; here and in St Thomas Street there are several characteristically attractive Georgian housefronts.

Return to the High Street, and its junction with **Jewry Street**. This street name recalls Winchester's Jewish ghetto; it was established at least by 1148, and here money-lenders and traders ran their businesses. They escaped the

16 *The clock (1713) of the former Guildhall projects over the High Street on an elaborately carved bracket.*

pogroms of 1189 and 1190 and lived peaceably with the citizens, servicing the financial needs of the Crown and suffering its occasional extortionate demands; but they did not escape the general expulsion of the Jews from England in 1290, and for seven hundred years the street name has been a record of past history.

A few paces down the High Street on the right the pretty 18th-century façade of the **Hampshire Chronicle's office** (**17**), to which Messrs Jacob and Johnson moved their newspaper business in 1813, is always bright with flowers above its twin bow windows.

17 *The* Hampshire Chronicle, *founded over two hundred years ago, preserves the old newspaper customs of printing only small advertisements on the front page and publishing all articles unsigned. Just inside the entrance to the office is the hand printing press of 1833 on which the paper used to be produced.*

The most striking figure of the High Street is the great **clock** (**16**) springing out in an ornamental wooden bracket from the upper storey of what is now Lloyds Bank. Here hangs the city's curfew bell, still sounded at eight o'clock every evening. The clock, and the statue of Queen Anne inscribed 'Anna Regina anno pacifico 1713', were presented by the two Members of Parliament for Winchester to adorn this building, which was originally the city's Guildhall. The date is significant, for in that year the Treaty of Utrecht brought to a triumphant end the long and expensive War of the Spanish Succession; Marlborough's victories had humbled Louis XIV and made Britain the dominant European power and mistress of Gibraltar. Winchester rejoiced in the return of peace and put up the Guildhall to celebrate, hoping Queen Anne might make Winchester a royal city again. Like Charles II before her, she nearly did, but, like Charles, she died too soon.

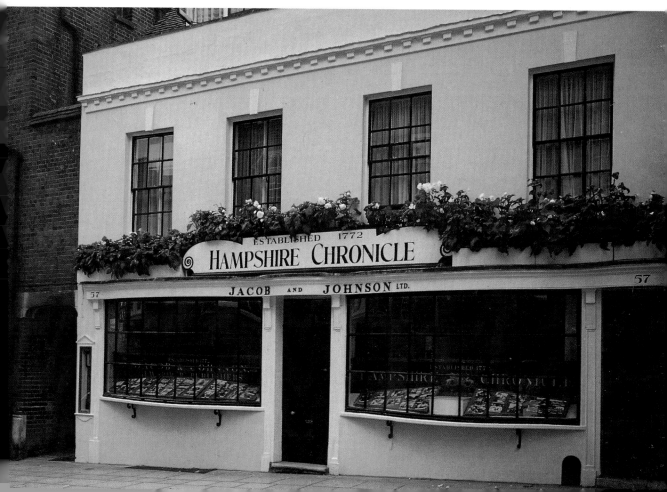

ESTABLISHED 1772
HAMPSHIRE CHRONICLE
57
JACOB AND JOHNSON LTD.
57

Opposite the old Guildhall and clock stands the timbered **God Begot House**. Much of the façade you see (**18**) belongs to an early-20th-century restoration, but a glance along the narrow alley that divides it from the Royal Oak Inn (once the boundary of the Jewish ghetto) reveals the projecting jettied work of the 16th-century timbered building (**19**). The name goes back to an old and curious story. In 1052 Queen Emma (mother of Edward the Confessor and later wife of Canute) bequeathed 'the manor of God Begot' to the Priory of St Swithun (i.e. the Saxon Cathedral). Until the Reformation this ancient manor remained a separate enclave within the city of Winchester. Its inhabitants were not citizens, nor did the citizens have any control over the manor: a malefactor could step over the boundary and defy his pursuers. After the Reformation the manor became the property of the dean and chapter of the Cathedral, and remained so until 1866, when it was sold. Until recently God Begot House was an attractive hotel, but modern fire regulations put a stop to that, and a shop now occupies it.

Further down, the National Westminster Bank (No. 105) presents to the street the decent façade of a substantial 18th-century apothecary's house, with a particularly pretty frieze above the ground-floor windows. On the opposite side stands the early-15th-century **Butter Cross** (**20**), or High Cross. Exactly when or why this cross was set up is not known; it appears not to be

a thank-offering for delivery from plague nor a monument to any event, but simply a city cross. It was greatly restored by Sir George Gilbert Scott in 1865.

The Butter Cross stands in a corner made by a high timbered 14th-century building (No. 42, The Spinning Wheel) and the beginning of the **Pentice**, a porticoed line of shops stretching down the High Street. Before you pass on, pause for a moment to imagine the family businesses that lined the High Street a century ago. No. 45, on the corner of Little Minster Street, was until 1980 the chemist's shop of Hunt and Co. (founded 1861), and halfway down the Pentice was Foster the tobacconist (founded 1878). The fascinating Victorian shop furnishings of both these businesses are splendidly displayed in the City Museum (upper floor), which can be visited on our way to the Cathedral.

The narrow passage behind the Butter Cross leads to the church of St Lawrence-in-the-Square, on the site of the Norman royal palace and mint (the church has Norman features and a very good selection of 18th-century wall monuments). Continuing past attractive shop façades and 18th-century town houses you come to **The Square**, and the first view of the Cathedral. Beyond the shops and the Vine Inn (**10**; on the right) runs **Great Minster Street**, a charming Georgian terrace, ending with the fine early-18th-century Minster House, once a private bank. On The Square to the left you will notice the timbered Eclipse Inn (so called because once the Sun Inn stood opposite); this is not an ancient hostelry, but the much-restored façade of the old rectory of St Lawrence. As you look along Market Street (between the Eclipse and the Museum), spare a thought for the Lady Alice Lisle. A victim of Judge Jeffreys' Bloody Assize, she was accused of harbouring traitors who had supported the Duke of Monmouth's anti-Catholic attempt to dethrone James II, and was beheaded in the street here in 1685.

The **Museum** is on the site of the old Market House, with the Cornmarket beyond it. The Museum is worth a visit before you go on to the Cathedral, not least because it contains an informative wooden model of the Saxon Cathedral (Oldminster) whose foundations you will be looking at as you make for the Cathedral's west door. In the Museum you can also see the surviving evidence of Roman Winchester, and of other periods in the city's history.

The Cathedral

As you approach the Cathedral through an avenue of young trees and first see the 14th-century west front (**21**), you have to remind yourself that the building was originally Norman and ruggedly Romanesque. Twin towers and stout round arches once brought this face of the Norman church some 40 feet further west.

Look first at the foundations of **Oldminster**, the Saxon Cathedral, which can be seen in the grass to the north (left) of the west door. Here Saxon bishops were enthroned from 676 onwards; here St Swithun was buried in 861; here St Ethelwold reformed and regularised the Benedictine rule, and was buried in 984. Behind you near the line of young trees stood King Alfred's Newminster (begun *c.* 900) until it was moved to Hyde Abbey in

1110. You are at the centre of what was once a great complex of Saxon religious buildings. Under royal patronage their inhabitants ensured the proper conduct of divine service, the pursuit of the arts and the continuity of architectural skills inherited from the Romans. All these were inherited in turn by the Norman Cathedral which rose alongside them, and which now stands here alone in its glory.

This Cathedral, like the Saxon Oldminster before it, was originally both the *cathedra* or seat of a bishop, and the monastic church of a Benedictine house under a prior. In 1070 both bishop and prior were French-speaking, French-educated Normans: Bishop William Walkelin and his brother Prior Simeon, kinsmen of William the Conqueror. It was Walkelin who in 1076 began the construction of a Norman building on the grand scale. Stone came in barges up the River Itchen from the Isle of Wight, and the Conqueror rashly promised Walkelin as much timber as he could fell and fetch in four days from Hempage Wood, in the royal forest out towards Alresford. Only one tree, so history relates, was left standing, and Walkelin had to do penance in sackcloth at the feet of an angry king before he was forgiven his presumptuous licence.

Within 14 years of building enough was standing for a great dedication ceremony to take place on 8 April 1093. The divine offices, celebrated the day before in the Saxon Oldminster, transferred without interruption to its Norman successor; the bones of St Swithun were moved to their new resting place, and Oldminster was dismantled.

Enter the Cathedral by the west door and stand for a moment with your back to the great west window, looking eastward down the longest **nave** in

24 *The deposition and entombment of Christ (c. 1200) in the Cathedral's Chapel of the Holy Sepulchre.*

23 *The Cathedral's 12th-century black marble font. On the south side, shown here, St Nicholas helps a poor man rescue his three daughters from prostitution by giving a dowry which enables the eldest to marry the man on the left. On the west side the saint restores to life three boys axed by a wicked innkeeper during a famine to make meat, and rescues drowning sailors from a well-ruddered ship.*

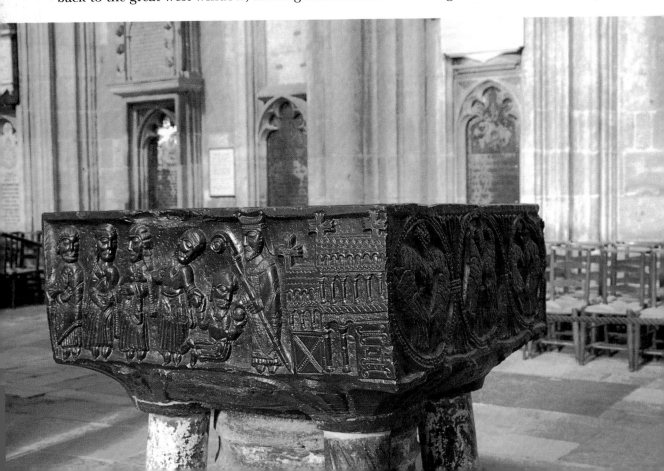

Europe (**22**). The Perpendicular arches and vaulting are the work of William of Wykeham (bishop of Winchester 1367–1404), who converted the solid Norman pillars and arches to the soaring and majestic Gothic style. The three storeys of dumpy Norman nave, triforium, and clerestory arches have been turned into a tall pointed nave arch, a blind gallery and a Perpendicular clerestory. Norman masonry was retained, and the pillars, more massive than one would expect in the Gothic style, have been given perpendicularity by an added cluster of vertical stonework. The principal shafts which run right up to support the vaulting are the original Norman masts. Wykeham's predecessor, Bishop Edington (1346–66), had begun the Gothic transformation, prompted perhaps by the imminent collapse of the Norman towers at the west end. The western façade (though not the great west window) is his work, as are the clerestory windows at the extreme west end. But the soaring majesty of the long nave is the work of Wykeham and his architect, William Wynford.

Now walk up the **north aisle**. At the fifth bay you will see in the floor the grave of Jane Austen, and a monument and commemorative window in the wall beside it. Her tombstone records the benevolent heart, sweet temper and extraordinary endowments of mind of this Hampshire lady, who finished her life's work in Winchester and whose novels (not mentioned on her grave) have made her a household name.

In the next bay stands the magnificent 800-year-old baptismal **font** (**23**) of black marble from Tournai in Belgium, possibly the gift of Henry de Blois (bishop of Winchester 1129–73). It is carved in the finest Romanesque style with birds and beasts and with scenes from the life of St Nicholas (Santa Claus), patron saint of children.

Move on to the **north transept**, looking first at the **Chapel of the Epiphany** on your left, and next at the transept itself. In both of these you see most clearly the massive, serene Norman style of Walkelin's cathedral. The chapel's stained glass is by the firm of William Morris. In the south-east corner of the transept is the entrance to the impressively complete **crypt**, which should not be missed if you are here in summer (it is closed in winter, being subject to flooding). The two Norman parts are Walkelin's work, echoing his transepts; the eastern part dates from 1189–1204, the period of the Lady Chapel above it.

The **Chapel of the Holy Sepulchre** faces the north transept in the solid masonry under the tower, without windows, as befits a sepulchre. It contains the most notable wall paintings in the Cathedral. They are late 12th and early 13th century, the best of their period in Britain, and stylistically they resemble the illustrations in the great Winchester Bible. On the east wall they portray the deposition and entombment of Christ (**24**); on the side wall, doubting Thomas, the entry into Jerusalem (above) and Mary Magdalene with Christ after the Resurrection. The west bay contains another deposition and entombment, formerly covering the one on the east wall and now lifted off. The Puritan preoccupation with idolatry led to these paintings being covered over, and their uncovering and restoration is a masterpiece of delicate 20th-century technical skill.

Mounting the steps to the **north presbytery aisle**, you pass on your right the **chantry of Stephen Gardiner** (**25**), bishop of Winchester in the difficult years of Henry VIII's Reformation, the reign of Edward VI and the

25 Looking back from the east end of the Cathedral down the north presbytery aisle. In the foreground, the early-14th-century tomb of Sir Arnold de Gaveston, father of Edward II's favourite Piers Gaveston and probably the first layman to be interred in the Cathedral; a veteran of the seventh crusade, he grasps the hilt of his sword, and a lion crouches to form his footrest. Beyond, the chantry of Stephen Gardiner (c. 1483–1555), appointed bishop of Winchester in 1531. His career illustrates the stormy fluctuations of English political and religious life in the 16th century. As secretary to Henry VIII he forwarded the king's divorce (which ushered in the English Reformation), served as ambassador to France, became Chancellor of Cambridge University and acquired supreme political influence. Under Edward VI he lost his bishopric and was imprisoned in the Tower of London for opposing doctrinal changes; on Mary's accession he was reinstated and became Lord Chancellor. Had he lived to Elizabeth's reign he would have suffered another reverse, for he had persuaded Parliament to declare her illegitimate and had been a fierce persecutor of Protestants.

26 *The vault of the Guardian Angels' Chapel, first painted with these designs in 1241, and most recently restored 1957–60.*

accession of the Catholic Queen Mary. An old-fashioned Catholic himself, he had crowned Queen Mary, as Lord Chancellor he had taken part in the negotiations that led to her marriage to Philip of Spain, and as bishop he conducted that marriage in Winchester Cathedral on 25 July 1554. The chair upon which Mary Tudor sat on her wedding day can be seen in his chantry.

You are now entering the **retrochoir**, where in 1202 Bishop Godfrey de Lucy began to extend the Cathedral eastwards, building over the Norman crypt a more spacious area to accommodate the growing cult of the shrine of St Swithun. (There are still tiles dating from *c.* 1230 on the floor.) Pilgrims came from great distances to visit the tomb of the saint, entering the monastic church through a door in the north transept. In 1538 Henry VIII's commissioners, with their frenzied zeal to destroy what they regarded as superstitious images, swooped on the shrine. Nothing was left to mark the place except a simple inscription, until, a thousand years after the saint's death, the Friends of the Cathedral set up the present shrine at the centre of the retrochoir in 1962.

Next look at the **chantry of William Waynflete**, which has a magnificently complicated ceiling. Waynflete was Lord Chancellor of

England, and bishop of Winchester 1447-86; before that he had been headmaster of Winchester College, where he had entertained Henry VI and shown him William of Wykeham's statutes. When Henry founded Eton College in 1440, he appointed Waynflete as its first provost, and when Cardinal Beaufort, bishop of Winchester, died in 1447, Henry instantly nominated Waynflete to succeed him. Back in Winchester, Waynflete again followed in the footsteps of William of Wykeham by founding a college in Oxford: his licence to found Magdalen College was granted in 1448.

The **Guardian Angels' Chapel** (**26**), north of the Lady Chapel, takes its name from its splendid painted roof, commissioned by Henry III in 1241, and last restored in 1960. This was the king known as Henry of Winchester, born and baptised here, and the builder of the Great Hall of the Castle. Notice also the very fine bronze and marble monument to Lord Portland, in a style looking far beyond the date of his death in 1634.

The **Lady Chapel**, planned (like the retrochoir) by Bishop de Lucy, was extended eastward in the reign of Henry VII. He was the first of the Tudors, winning his throne from Richard III at the Battle of Bosworth. It was important to him to establish the validity and antiquity of his line; he therefore named his first-born Arthur, and was careful to have him born and baptised in Winchester. It was to celebrate this christening in September 1486 that the Lady Chapel was extended. From the outside it is

27 *Emblems of Bishop Fox (bishop of Winchester 1501–28) on the vault of the choir, which is largely his work.*

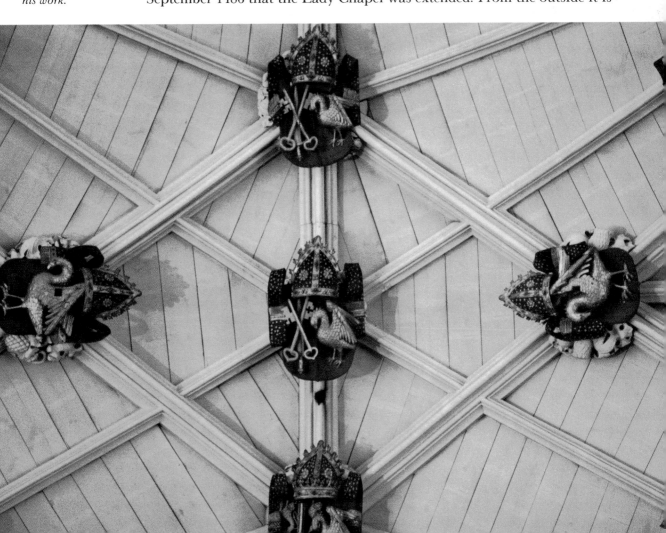

easy to see where the Tudor addition meets de Lucy's 13th-century east end. The painted panels, showing miracles performed by the Virgin, are copies of the originals preserved underneath, commissioned by Prior Silkstede *c.* 1500. Beyond the Lady Chapel to the south is the **chantry of Bishop Langton**, who died in 1500 just before he was to be enthroned as archbishop of Canterbury. The elaborate oak panelling dates from the building of the chapel.

Cardinal Henry Beaufort, great-uncle of Henry VI, bishop of Winchester 1404–47, wanted to be buried near St Swithun; his wish was granted, and **Cardinal Beaufort's chantry** was built with befitting grandeur. The sad burning of Joan of Arc has to be held against him, and since 1923 a gilt statue of the Maid has stood opposite the Cardinal's chantry, her gaze averted. We shall see the kindlier side of Beaufort in his splendid work at St Cross.

Finest of all the chantries is the **chantry of Bishop Fox**, in the **south presbytery aisle**. He died in 1528, a frail old man, having done much to beautify the Cathedral in his 27 years as bishop. The **flying buttresses** outside at the east end are his work, as are the **east window** and the **presbytery screens**. Statesman, church reformer and academic, he was the founder of Corpus Christi College in Oxford and Chancellor of Cambridge University. The sculpted cadaver in his chantry is a reminder of the fate that awaits us all, even one who has been bishop of four major sees.

It is now time to move into the **presbytery** and **choir**. Behind the high altar you see the great stone **reredos** (**28**) of the late 15th century. The figures in it, like the bones of the Saxon kings in the mortuary chests above Fox's screens to either side of it, were despoiled and scattered at the Reformation. The Restoration saw the Saxon bones decently collected and replaced, and 19th-century statuary now fills the reredos.

The superb woodwork of the **choir stalls** (**29**), alive with men, animals and birds, is dated to 1308. Tip up the seats to study their misericords (the ledges on which medieval monks used to support themselves during the long services), carved with a wealth of humorous figures – animal, human and mythical. On the floor between the choir stalls stands the crude unmarked tomb of King William Rufus. The pulpit belongs to the age of Prior Silkstede (1498–1524), and bears his name and a pun on it – carved skeins of silk. The sanctuary carpet is part of one which lay in Westminster Abbey at the coronation of King George VI in 1937.

To reach the **south transept** you pass through metal **grille gates** of great antiquity: believed to be the oldest metal gates in England, they were made for the Cathedral in the 12th or 13th century. In the transept itself you see again the sturdy Norman work of Walkelin's time. The southernmost **chapel of Prior Silkstede**, the last but three of the priors of the Benedictine monastery, contains the grave of the fisherman writer Izaak Walton, who was buried here in 1683. The Walton window was given in 1914 by fishermen from all over England and America. In the bottom light of the right-hand side Walton sits reading with his fishing tackle beside him, and behind him flows the River Itchen, rich in trout, with the round hump of St Catherine's Hill beyond. The legend below, 'study to be quiet' (*1 Thessalonians* 4:11), is one of his favourite texts, quoted in his renowned *The Compleat Angler*.

28 *The east end of the choir, looking towards the high altar, reredos and east window. On either side are the presbytery screens, surmounted by mortuary chests containing the bones of Saxon kings and bishops (see also p. 13).*

In the opposite corner of the transept a staircase rises to the **Cathedral Library**, a 12th-century room reconstructed in 1668. The treasures displayed include the Cathedral's most precious possession, the four-volume illuminated Winchester Bible of the 12th century.

Walking now westward along the **south aisle**, pause to look at Sir George Gilbert Scott's choir screen, a 19th-century work in wood which perhaps chimes more happily with the choir stalls behind it than did its 17th-century predecessor, a classical stone screen designed by Inigo Jones. You come next to the **chantry of Bishop Edington**, Wykeham's predecessor, who began the reconstruction of the nave in the Gothic style: his coat of arms adorns some of the bosses of the nave's great lierne vault.

Over the door halfway along the south side is a window given by United States citizens to mark their respect for the character of King George V. It was unveiled in July 1938 by the American ambassador, Joseph Kennedy, father of the President.

The last of the great chantries is the **chantry of William of Wykeham**, Lord Chancellor, bishop of Winchester, and founder of New College, Oxford, and of Winchester College. He lies in the fourth bay of the nave which he so gloriously reconstructed, with three monkish clerkly figures at his feet. Whether it be true or not, it is nice to remember the story of the Wykehamist Nathaniel Fiennes defending the tomb of his old school's founder from the attentions of his own Cromwellian troops (see p.16).

Leave by the south door to look at the Close and the exterior of the

30 *A view through the buttresses added to the south wall of the nave in 1905–12 to save the Cathedral from collapse.*

29 *The Cathedral's magnificent choir stalls (1308). In the foreground is the unmarked tomb of the despotic William Rufus (1056–1100), who succeeded his father, William the Conqueror, in 1087.*

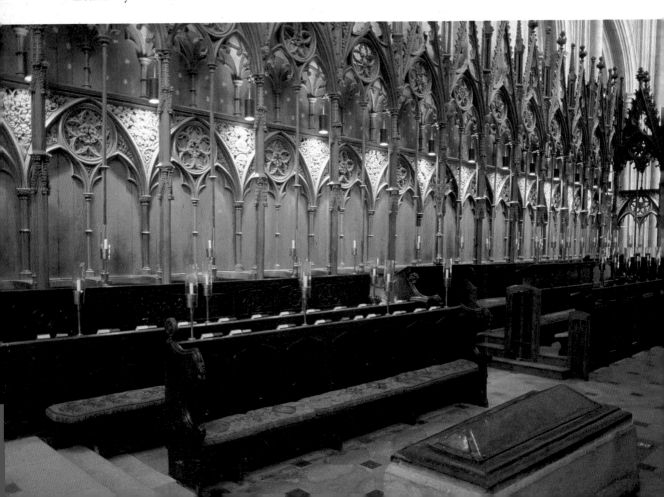

Cathedral. Immediately you find yourself between two of ten **buttresses (30)** that run the length of the south wall, and look as if they have stood there forever. In fact they belong to the years 1905–12 when the Cathedral's foundations, particularly along the south side of the retrochoir, were seen to be slipping. The great mass of the Norman walls rested on a raft of beech trunks below the water-table, and these rested in turn on a peat bed which was sagging, compressed by the huge weight above. There was nothing for it but to replace the peat with concrete sandbags under solid concrete, and to replace the tree trunks with brick.

The massive work was planned by the architects J.B. Colson and T.G. Jackson and the engineer Francis Fox, overseen by the Clerk of the Works E. Long. The services of a diver were needed, and off and on for more than six years William Walker worked underground and underwater in the old-fashioned round helmet and weighted boots of naval divers. His work caught the imagination of press and public, and he is commemorated today by a plaque on the west wall and a statue in the retrochoir. By his labour the Cathedral was saved.

Further safety was secured by the addition of the ten buttresses, which give to the south wall the support once assured by the Norman cloister which abutted this side of the Cathedral and stretched in a square across the grass. They are a triumph of design, and do much for the rhythm of this south face, now denuded of its cloister. An inscription on the westernmost

31 *No. 9 The Close, with the pinnacles of the Cathedral's west front behind.*

The 13th-century porch of the Deanery, with the 15th-century prior's hall to the left and the 17th-century long gallery to the right; behind, the Cathedral's Norman tower and south transept and Gothic east end.

buttress modestly says, in Latin (and more elegantly), 'with these ten little buttresses the church was propped up in 1912'.

As you stand looking south across the **Close**, fill it in your mind's eye with the range of monastic buildings that once stood here. Next to the south transept the round arches and cushion capitals of the entrance to the Norman **chapter house** still remain. Between them and the Deanery stood the monks' dormitory, and the Deanery itself was the prior's lodging. The refectory ran from the Deanery to No. 10 The Close, completing the south side of the square. In the 16th century these buildings disappeared, through either the neglect or the reforming zeal of Bishop Horne. For nearly five centuries monks had lived and worked here under the Benedictine rule, studying, teaching and manufacturing such masterpieces as the Winchester Bible.

Pause at the front of the **Deanery** (**32**). The superb 13th-century porch, with three Gothic arches, is rib-vaulted inside. The 15th-century Prior's Hall still exists in the grey stone western end of the house, and the dean's study is in the 17th-century red brick long gallery extending to the east. As you look at the building, with the squat Norman tower of the Cathedral rising behind it, it speaks to you of the strangely easy transition in 1541 from a monastery headed by a prior to a cathedral with a dean and chapter.

Opposite is the attractive low Georgian façade of the **Judge's Lodging**, originally of the 17th century, and to the west runs picturesque **Dome Alley**, its brick houses built by the dean and chapter in 1663. Here at No. 7 Izaak

Walton died in 1683. Nos. 9 and 10 The Close are in 17th-century stone, and No. 10 retains the medieval vaulted undercroft of the range of monastic buildings that once filled the western side of the Close.

The **Pilgrims' School**, its Georgian front cladding a 17th-century building, forms the eastern edge of the Close. A conventional preparatory school as well as the Cathedral's choir school, it takes its name from the flint-faced 14th-century **Pilgrims' Hall** adjoining it to the north. Here, it is said, pilgrims to the shrine of St Swithun were lodged – under the earliest known English hammerbeam roof, probably the work of Thomas of Witney in 1325.

The early-16th-century timber-framed stable block (**33**) runs south to the three timbered gables of **Cheyney Court** and to **St Swithun's Gate** (**34**), both 15th century. As you leave the Close by this gate into St Swithun Street, the grey flint wall of the Cathedral precinct is on your right, and the city wall runs behind the houses on your left.

From the Cathedral to St Cross

Kingsgate (**35**) stands on the line of the city wall at the north end of Kingsgate Street; the windows above it are those of the atmospheric small church of **St Swithun-upon-Kingsgate** (first recorded 1263). The present gate belongs to the 14th century, but has Roman origins. The two smaller pavement side arches were added in the 18th century.

Passing through Kingsgate, you see in front of you the narrow run of

33 The 16th-century prior's stable block in the Cathedral Close, now part of the Pilgrims' School.

34 Looking through St Swithun's Gate, out of the Cathedral Close, towards Kingsgate.

Kingsgate Street, a rewarding view of pretty house fronts with Georgian bow windows and decorative doorcases. Turning left into **College Street**, you have on your left the backs of Cheyney Court. On the right at No. 8 (**36**) is the house where **Jane Austen** died. She was the seventh of the eight children of the Rector at Steventon, near Basingstoke, where she spent her first 16 years. Her brothers had all left home (two to become admirals) when the family moved first to Bath and then to Southampton. In 1809 Jane and her mother and her devoted sister Cassandra settled at Chawton, near Alton, where she wrote her last novels (see p. 74).

In December 1816 her nephew Edward finished his studies at Winchester College, and received a characteristic letter from his Aunt Jane: 'I give you Joy of having left Winchester. Now you may own, how miserable you were there; now, it will gradually all come out – your Crimes & your Miseries – how often you went up by the Mail to London & threw away Fifty Guineas at a Tavern, & how often you were on the point of hanging yourself – restrained only, as some illnatured aspersion upon poor old Winton has it, by the want of a Tree within some miles of the City.'

In May 1817, her health failing, she and her sister Cassandra took lodgings at 'Mrs David's, College Street, Winton' to seek the medical advice of Mr Lyford. On 27 May she wrote to her nephew: 'Mr Lyford says he will

36 *The house in College Street in which Jane Austen spent the last weeks of her life, while working on her final novel,* Persuasion.

35 *The present Kingsgate, with the church of St Swithun-upon-Kingsgate forming its upper storey, dates from the 14th century. During the Commonwealth St Swithun's was let to a man who lived in one end of the church and kept his pigs at the other. There has been a city gate on this site since Roman times.*

37 *Winchester College: the 14th-century statue of the Virgin and Child placed by the Founder on Outer Gate. William of Wykeham dedicated his College 'to the honour and glory of God and of the glorious Virgin Mary His Mother'.*

cure me, & if he fails, I shall draw up a Memorial and lay it before the Dean & Chapter, & have no doubt of redress from that Pious, Learned, and Disinterested Body. Our Lodgings are very comfortable. We have a neat little Drawing room with a Bow-window overlooking Dr. Gabell's garden.' In the neat little drawing room with the bow window on the first floor she put the finishing touches to *Persuasion*, and penned some light verses about Winchester Races and St Swithun's tendency to rain upon them in July. There was time for no more. Mr Lyford's attention was of no avail, and three days after St Swithun's Day, on 18 July 1817, she died here, aged 42.

In later years No. 8 was well known to the young gentlemen of Winchester College for Octo La Croix's ices and pastries, and his shop window can still be seen to the left of the front door. Like the other houses in College Street, No. 8 is now occupied by a College master.

Further down Kingsgate Street you come to the long grey medieval frontage of **Winchester College**. Founded in 1382 by William of Wykeham, bishop of Winchester and Lord Chancellor of England, its first stone was laid in 1387, the year in which Chaucer began his *Canterbury Tales*. The fortress-like exterior serves to remind us how troubled those days were. Only with the support of a royal charter and the blessing of the Holy See could such a work have been undertaken at such a time.

Wykeham had already founded New College in Oxford, and a school was

38 *Winchester College has used its original buildings since its foundation in the 14th century. Here scholars, in the traditional black gowns which distinguish them from other pupils, assemble in Chamber Court on the stairs to Hall (its windows are on the left).*

52

40 *The wooden vault of Winchester College Chapel, built by Hugh Herland for the Founder, and repainted in 1952 in its original colours.*

39 *The west window of Thurbern's Chantry, the south aisle of the Chapel, filled with the original 1390s glass of the east window (which now contains 19th-century copies). Bottom left, the Founder kneels to the Virgin and Child; bottom right, Richard II, who granted the foundation charter, kneels to God the Father.*

the second part of his plan to replenish the literate, clerkly, priestly class required for the proper administration of the realm in the Middle Ages. The buildings are the plant thought suitable by a rich, worldly-wise but pious statesman for the instruction of 70 poor and needy scholars in the study of letters and the art of grammar – the basis of all the arts and sciences (at least in the Middle Ages). This admirable process has continued without interruption for six centuries, and Wykeham's 70 scholars still occupy the College he built for them, and enjoy his bounty. They are joined now by some 580 Commoners (*commensales* – sharers of tables) who live in ten boarding houses (mostly Victorian).

In a niche over **Outer Gate** stands a 14th-century statue of Our Lady (**37**), to whom Wykeham dedicated both his colleges; astonishingly, it has survived intact. As you pass under this finely vaulted gate you are entering a compact, secure and self-sufficient medieval complex, whose **Outer Court** contained a granary, a brewhouse (now a library) and stables, well watered by two streams.

Middle Gate, again finely vaulted, leads to **Chamber Court** (**38**), round which lived Wykeham's collegiate community of warden, ten fellows, two masters, three chaplains, three lay clerks and 16 quiristers (choristers) and the 70 scholars. All these positions established at the original foundation still exist, though only the 70 scholars and the Second Master now live in College.

Wykeham's **Chapel** dominates the south side of the quadrangle, built expensively in Bere stone, while the other sides of Chamber Court are in

flint-faced bonded rubble. The Chapel's fine ceiling (**40**), in wood with a lierne vault, almost a fan vault, was made by Wykeham's master carpenter Hugh Herland, who later built the great roof of Westminster Hall. It was repainted in 1952 with a reproduction of the Founder's original colours. The great Jesse east window and the side windows are 19th-century copies of the glass put up in the 1390s by Wykeham's glazier, Thomas of Oxford. Blackened and corroded by the years, the old glass was removed in 1820 and dispersed – a sad loss, for the whole Chapel is designed, in the manner of Perpendicular builders, for the display of fine stained glass. Happily some of Thomas' glass has been recovered and glows again in the west window under the tower (**39**). The panelling and pews belong to 1913–21 (they allow a building designed for the devotion of 105 people to accommodate more than 300), but the misericords are the Founder's: look for a hawk with a duck, a shepherd, a pelican in her piety, and a cripple (with pieces of wood tied to his hands and feet to help him move around).

The rest of the south range of Chamber Court contains **Hall** above, and **Seventh Chamber** (the original schoolroom) below. A little lobby in the west range contains the famous Trusty Servant painting – a strangely medieval concept of the qualities of the perfect servant, expressed in a wealth of emblems (and explained in Latin elegiacs and in English). Originally 16th century and much repainted, the figure in its present form, in blue Windsor livery, was done by William Cave in 1809.

A little passage by the west end of Chapel leads out of Chamber Court, and you are confronted by a square brick and stone building in Wren's style

41 Winchester College's War Cloister (1922–4), a monument planned by Headmaster Rendall and a hundred Old Wykehamists at Amiens shortly before the Battle of Cambrai during World War I. The memorial fund established to build it also endowed bursaries for the sons of Wykehamists killed in the war.

(but not his work), with a statue (1692) of the Founder over the door by C.G. Cibber. This is **School**, built by Warden Nicholas in 1687 as a schoolroom for the growing number of boys, and still retaining a little of the furniture of that age at its west end. Numbers had grown again by the 19th century, and the present classrooms, in Flint Court (behind your right shoulder as you look at School), are by Butterfield (1867–70). He was remodelling what had been a sort of barracks lived in by Commoners until the 1860s, when they moved out to their present boarding houses. Life was rugged for schoolboys then, and the buildings of 'Old Commoners' were rugged too. 'Mr Butterfield,' said the Warden when he saw the new classrooms, 'you have made a silk purse out of a sow's ear'.

Both School and the Flint Court classrooms are mere upstarts compared to the Founder's old schoolroom in Seventh Chamber. Equally venerable are his barrel-ribbed **Cloisters** south of Chapel, fit for the monkish perambulations of his fellows and scholars and for the holding of classes in summer (still called Cloister Time). Surprisingly, a building occupies the middle of the garth – there can be few other examples of such an intrusion, but this is a very happy one. John Fromond, steward of the College Manors, died in 1420 and bequeathed money for a chantry chapel, where masses were to be sung for him. The charming **Fromond chantry** is superbly vaulted and windowed, and above it a small library houses a collection of College memorabilia.

Walk now across **Meads** behind School, under colossal ancient plane trees; the encircling wall, made from the stones of St Elizabeth's College

42 The remaining wing of the residence built by Bishop Morley at Wolvesey in the 17th century, now the palace of the bishops of Winchester. To the right is the 15th-century chapel, formerly the chapel of Wolvesey Castle, which was demolished during the Commonwealth.

(destroyed at the Reformation), contains little niches where candles are lit at the end of the Christmas term. From here you see the round arches and oriel windows of Basil Champneys' **Memorial Buildings**, completed in 1890 to mark the fifth centenary of the founding, and beside it the entrance to Sir Herbert Baker's **War Cloister** (41). This gracious memorial commemorates the five hundred Wykehamists who died in the First World War, and serves as a lovely thoroughfare for the Commoners going between their houses and the classrooms.

A little 17th-century **Sick House** for the scholars (still used as such) stands beyond Memorial Buildings, planned to be well away from School. Its demure face (1656) is inscribed, in Hebrew, 'Bethesda' (a healing pool in Jerusalem, *John* 5:2), and must look with some distress at Basil Champneys' undulating Italianate balcony; but the pain with which its Georgian back regards the old Sanatorium of 1884–93 must be greater. This strange pair of turreted Amboise chateaux in red brick, having failed to fall down, are now 'listed buildings', and have been made marginally less horrid by their conversion into an Art School.

After a glance at St Catherine's Hill, which rises to the south east, it is time to retrace your steps through Chamber Court and back to College Street. Just before you pass through Outer Gate, you see on your right the flint façade of the **Warden's Lodgings** (1830), where he and the fellows (the governing body) hold their meetings. The medieval celibate wardens had lived over Middle Gate, but the Reformation brought matrimony and the

43 Wolvesey Castle ruins: a view of the north end of the great hall.

44 *On the way to St Cross: the water meadows of the River Itchen on the south-east side of the city.*

need for a family house. Behind the façade is a building dating from 1597 and remodelled in 1692. The buttressed street side of the Lodgings bears the dates 1597 and 1730.

Walking over the stream Logie, you come on your left to **Wolvesey** (**42**), the home of the bishops of Winchester. This is an area rich in the history of bishops and monarchs, and it is simplest to start at the end of the story. As you peep through the gates of Wolvesey you are looking at the single surviving wing of a baroque palace built by Bishop Morley in the 1680s – and designed not by Wren, as is often supposed, but by his contemporary Sir Thomas Fitch, a leading master bricklayer who had executed important commissions in Portsmouth and London. Since 1928 this wing has been the sole home of bishops of Winchester, who once ruled their vast diocese from their six castles at Farnham, Downton, Taunton, Merdon, Bishop's Waltham and Wolvesey, or from Winchester House at Southwark. In the grounds to the east of the house you can enter the imposing ruins of a Saxon and Norman episcopal castle. To trace the story from castles to a relatively modest house, we must go back to the beginning.

Saxon bishops lodged in the monastery complex of Oldminster until Ethelwold (bishop 963–84) reformed the Saxon monasteries into proper closed orders, where there was no place for a diocesan bishop and his increasing staff. He therefore built a bishop's hall here on the open ground between Oldminster and the south-east corner of the Roman wall, bounded to the north by Nunnaminster, the Saxon nunnery which, from Alfred's time until the Reformation, occupied the area now bounded by the Broadway and Colebrook Street.

The second Norman bishop, William Giffard (1107–29), built over the Saxon site, but it was the third Norman bishop who constructed here a castle on the grand scale. This was Henry de Blois, grandson of the Conqueror, brother of King Stephen, Abbot of Glastonbury, a Papal Legate, and the greatest man in the land.

Apart from grandeur, riches and power, Henry de Blois had civilised tastes of the highest quality; he was a patron of the arts and a great builder. Here he built magnificently, and most of what you see are the ruins of his work – a castle of 38 rooms with four ranges round a central courtyard, the whole strongly fortified. 'Castle', not 'palace', is the right word, for Henry was building at the time of the Stephen–Matilda wars, in which his own troops were actively (and ambiguously) engaged. During the struggle he destroyed the Norman palace (on the site of St Lawrence's church) and used the stones for additions to Wolvesey.

Henry de Blois' castle became increasingly important after his death; in fact it lasted five hundred years. The royal castle by the Westgate was damaged by fire at Easter 1302 and never occupied by royalty again; from then on, when kings came to Winchester, they lodged at Wolvesey, and the bishops would leave their other castles and come here to receive them.

Though capital and court had long ago moved to London, Winchester kept its place in the hearts of English kings, and these ruins were once the scene of royal grandeur and festivity. Here William of Wykeham (who spent 16 Easters at Wolvesey) received Richard II when he attended the Parliament session in 1393, and Henry IV in 1403 when he came to marry Joan of Navarre in the Cathedral. At Wolvesey Henry V met the French Ambassadors before Agincourt, and Henry VI stayed here with his great-uncle, Cardinal Beaufort, and with Bishop Waynflete when he was planning the foundation of Eton on the pattern of Winchester College. Richard III was here during his struggle with Bolingbroke, and at Wolvesey Queen Mary first met Philip II of Spain before their marriage in the Cathedral on 25 July 1554.

But the day of castles was passing. After the Civil War Wolvesey declined – expensive to maintain and no longer appropriate. Its glory departed, its stones were used for repairs to roads and walls. You can still make out the gatehouse, north-east tower, garderobe tower and keep, and parts of the great east hall, especially the north wall, with late Romanesque detail suggestive of its former splendour (43).

Bishop Morley's new baroque palace faced south, stretching across your vision as you look through the gates. At each end wings projected northward, away from you and out of sight from the road. The surviving west wing adjoins the earlier Bishop's chapel, which probably dates from the 15th century and has Norman foundations.

After 1721 the bishops lived solely at Farnham, and Wolvesey was neglected. Again repairs proved too expensive, and in 1786 Bishop North demolished all but the west wing. For what remained little use was found until the present century. In 1927 the huge diocese of Winchester was split up by the creation of the sees of Guildford and Portsmouth, and it seemed right to Bishop Theodore Woods to move from Farnham to Winchester.

45 *Beaufort Tower, the gateway to the medieval almshouse of St Cross, rising massively behind the 15th-century range of the main quadrangle. To the left is the Elizabethan east range.*

The architect W.D. Caroe was commissioned to make the derelict west wing into a suitable see house for the bishop, and so it has been since 1928. After many vicissitudes the bishop of Winchester is back in the home of his Saxon predecessors.

It is now time to take a walk through the **water meadows (2, 44)** from Wolvesey to Henry de Blois' other great foundation, the Hospital of St Cross. Choose if possible the mists of an early September evening, for you will be passing between limpid chalk streams where Izaak Walton angled for trout, and where Keats composed his ode *To Autumn*. In August 1819 the 24-year-old poet came to Winchester, 'chiefly for the purpose', he wrote to his sister Fanny, 'of being near a tolerable Library'. He did not find one to satisfy him, but even so he decided 'it is the pleasantest Town I ever was in', and he finished *Lamia* and *The Eve of St Agnes*. Consumption was already upon him, and he was to die two years later in Rome. He loved Winchester for its Cathedral, its fine trees and 'the most beautiful streams about I ever saw – full of trout'. His only regret was that 'I have not been well enough to bathe, though I live now close to delicious bathing'.

In a letter of 5 September to his publisher, John Taylor, we find his health improving – 'there is on one side of the city a dry chalky down where the air is worth sixpence a pint'. Autumn was his season; he walked every day for an hour before dinner. On 21 September he wrote to his friend Reynolds, 'How beautiful the season is now – How fine the air. A temperate sharpness about it'. The 'season of mists and mellow fruitfulness', when the fields were golden with stubble, was much to be preferred to the 'chilly green of the Spring'. 'This struck me so much in my Sunday's walk that I composed upon it'. No visit to Winchester is complete without a walk in Keats' footsteps through the meadows, where coot and moorhen paddle in the chalk streams edged with comfrey, monkey flower, willow herb and meadowsweet. The hump of St Catherine's Hill rises on your left; continue past trim allotments where the tower of the **Hospital of St Cross** comes into view, and approach the encircling wall across a pasture meadow.

Almshouses in Britain are nearly always attractive, and at St Cross you will find not only the oldest charitable institution in the country, but also without question the most beautiful. The foundation is the work of two men, separated by two centuries; both held the bishopric of Winchester for 44 years, both had royal connections, both were men of immense wealth and power in the kingdom. They have already been encountered several times in this survey of Winchester, whose fabric and history they were instrumental in creating: Henry de Blois, grandson of the Conqueror, brother of King Stephen, and bishop of Winchester 1129-73; and Cardinal Beaufort, son of John of Gaunt, half-brother of Henry IV, and bishop of Winchester 1404-47.

Henry de Blois founded his almshouse for 13 of the poor of Christ in meadows to the south of Winchester once laid waste by the Danes. By his bounty the 13 brethren were to be housed, clothed and fed within the Hospital. A further hundred poor persons were to be 'received at the hour of dinner', and they fed daily in Hundred Men's Hall just inside the outer gate, where stables now stand.

Henry de Blois' foundation opened in 1151, and the church was begun. Two papal bulls confirmed the rights to the property and arranged tithes to

46 *A panorama of St Cross from the south-west, its buildings spanning the years 1150–1500; left to right, the high chimneys of the brothers' quarters, the Hall and part of Beaufort's Tower, and the church.*

support it. Two more bulls (in Henry's long life he communicated with four popes) placed the management of the foundation in the hands of the Knights Hospitaller of St John of Jerusalem, an arrangement later reversed by a fifth pope, but reinstated by a royal charter of Richard I. Finally, in 1204, the right to appoint the Master of St Cross was transferred to the bishop of Winchester, who holds it to this day.

Cardinal Beaufort refounded the Hospital in 1446, and work continued during the chaos of the Wars of the Roses. To de Blois' foundation for the very poor he added provision for nobility or gentlefolk who had lost their wealth. The brethren of the Noble Order of Poverty still wear claret-coloured caps and gowns, while the original brothers are in the black ordained by the Knights Hospitaller. All wear a silver cross, which is passed to a new brother at the death of the wearer.

The buildings you see now are Beaufort's work. The influence of the architecture of Oxford and Cambridge colleges – and indeed of Winchester College – is plain to see. An outer gate (**45**) leads to an outer court flanked by functional buildings: stable and kitchen to the right, and brewhouse to the left. Here de Blois' hundred men formerly took their daily meal. A monumental gateway, the Beaufort Tower, leads into the main open quadrangle and contains the porter's lodge. Here you may still ask for, and receive, the Wayfarer's Dole – a small horn of beer and a piece of bread – in pious memory of de Blois' plan to feed the poor.

The brethren live college-wise on the staircases that form the long high-chimneyed western range of the quadrangle. Off each staircase live four

47 *The monastic simplicity of the Hall in which the brothers of St Cross used to eat together.*

brothers in sets of three rooms each. They used to dine communally in Hall (**47**) next to Beaufort's Tower; they still worship together daily in the Church of St Cross, ministered to by the Master, who now lives in his 19th-century flint Lodge beyond the outer gate.

The noble **Church of St Cross** (**49**), begun in the 12th century and finished in the 13th, brings together Norman and Early English styles, and manifests the transition between them. Building began at the east end, and there and in the north transept the meeting of styles is at its most exuberant. Work went on in the 14th century (the west window, clerestory windows and nave vault); the 15th century added glass to east windows and south transept; the 16th century added brasses and the chancel woodwork, and in the 19th century Butterfield was busy restoring. The squat tower looks Norman in its top storey, echoing the shape of the Cathedral's, but it belongs to the late 13th century, and was rebuilt in 1384.

Returning to the open quadrangle, you see on the eastern side a pretty low-arched Tudor cloister in wood (**48**), and through it a door leads to a garden of herb-beds and old-fashioned flowers, bordered by the water meadows, where the middle distance is filled by the rising roundness of St Catherine's Hill.

The beauty of the site contrasts with its history. A proper trusteeship of the charitable funds did not begin until the late 19th century, and for many years St Cross suffered the depredations of corrupt Masters. An unfortunate clause in some statutes of the Hospital drawn up in 1696 declares that when the Master has discharged all proper dues, he can claim any surplus of the revenues for himself. This led in the 18th century to further scandals of

48 *St Cross' Tudor cloister adjoins the church's 12th-century north transept.*

absentee Masters who regarded their office as a lucrative sinecure, gained by nepotism and then neglected. Matters came to a head toward the end of the 18th century. In 1781 the Prime Minister, Lord North, appointed his brother, the Hon. Brownlow North, as bishop of Winchester. In 1807 the bishop appointed his son, Francis, as Master of St Cross, an office he was to hold and neglect for nearly 50 years, succeeding to the earldom of Guildford in the middle of his tenure.

The decay of the Hospital and the neglect and peculation of the errant Earl were revealed to the press by the Rev. Harold Holloway, and expensive legal action followed which led in 1855 to the resignation of the Earl and the bankruptcy of the Hospital. Not for the last time, investigative journalism had scotched a scandal and left a muddle. Slowly and painfully, with the help of conscientious Masters and of much public goodwill, the Hospital recovered to become again a haven for the elderly in beautiful surroundings.

Anthony Trollope's first Barchester novel, *The Warden*, appeared in 1855, the year of the final débacle of St Cross, and its story of the Master of an ancient almshouse driven by public criticism to resign must owe much to contemporary press comment on St Cross (though Trollope's gentle Master has nothing in common with the Earl of Guildford). The ragamuffin son of literary but feckless and impecunious parents, Trollope had been educated briefly at Winchester College, and St Cross may claim to have given him the first idea for the context in which his Barchester characters were to begin to develop (though Barchester's chief inspiration is Salisbury).

St Cross is in many ways the right place at which to end a visit to ancient Winchester. Here is the best view of St Catherine's Hill, its defensive trench around the Celtic settlement clearly visible. Here among the chalk streams the Danes devastated the ancient village of Sparkford, but they never reached Winchester, thanks perhaps to St Swithun and certainly to King Alfred. Here the great figures of Norman and medieval England – Henry de Blois, William of Wykeham and Cardinal Beaufort – left their mark. At St Cross little has changed since those days, and after taking the Wayfarer's Dole you leave with the air of medieval England around you, and the taste of the Middle Ages upon your lips.

But a few more things of interest and charm remain to be seen, and you should now retrace your steps through the water meadows to Wolvesey (for variety, begin with the pleasant Back Street opposite the Hospital entrance). Take a stroll along Riverside Walk through the **Weirs** (**50**), with a splendid stretch of the medieval **city walls** on your left, and on your right the mill stream of the River Itchen. Passing pretty gardens, you will see in front of you the little **City Bridge** (reconstructed in 1813) and beyond it the old **City Mill** (**51**, dated 1744; now a Youth Hostel belonging to the National Trust). Here you see why Roman and pre-Roman Winchester came to be situated where it is. You are now at the bottom of the chalk valley where the river is most easily crossed, and the town spreads over the higher ground to your left. Much of the arrangement of medieval non-royal Winchester can be adduced here.

Turn right and cross the bridge. You are now in that part of the city known as the **Soke**, an area under the jurisdiction of the bishop's court, and

49 *The church of St Cross, chapel of the brothers of the almshouse: a view of the chancel and north transept showing details of the Romanesque architecture and decoration.*

therefore separate from the rest of the city, and technically free from the Corporation's restrictive trade regulations. This freedom brought much grist to the bishop's mill, but far more important was his control of St Giles' Fair, from which the hill rising to the east of the town takes its name.

The bishop's right to hold a fair here goes back to the 11th century and the time of King William Rufus. Originally a three-day affair straddling St Giles' Day (1 September), the fair grew into a great international trading event lasting more than two weeks – the medieval version of a modern trade fair. Manufacturers and dealers came from all over England and the Continent to display their wares, bringing wool and cloth from English merchants, silks and spices which had reached Europe from the ancient caravan routes, and wines from the European mainland. This annual influx of English and foreign merchants made medieval Winchester known far beyond the bounds of Wessex, and indeed beyond the shores of England. But the Black Death and the plague years of the 14th century dealt the fair a blow from which it never recovered. Already London was a greater centre of trade, and soon Winchester's name was forgotten by the merchants from France, Spain and the Low Countries.

Two ancient churches survive in the Soke. In Chesil Street **St Peter Chesil**, now used as a theatre workshop, has clear 13th-century features in the tower and interior. On the opposite side of the street on the corner with Bridge Street stands its **Old Rectory (53)**, now a restaurant, restored round the timber framing dating from c. 1450.

A short walk up St John's Street, also in the Soke, is rewarding, for on your right you soon come to **Tudor House**, its timber frame jettied out over

50 The Weirs, between the city walls and the River Itchen – a favourite Wintonian stroll, less than 5 minutes from the city centre.

51 The 18th-century City Mill, at the eastern end of the High Street. A mill is mentioned on this site in the 12th-century Winchester Domesday Book. Until the Reformation, the mill belonged to the priory of Wherwell (near Andover); it was granted to the city by royal charter in 1554. The adjoining City Bridge spans the Itchen where St Swithun first bridged it in the 9th century.

52-54 *Above left, the oldest parish church in Winchester, St John the Baptist (12th century); above right, the oldest residence in the city, Blue Boar House (14th century); and below left, the former rectory of St Peter Chesil (15th century), all in the ancient part of Winchester at the foot of St Giles' Hill known as the Soke. The word means an area under special jurisdiction, and until 1835 this part of the city was governed by the bishop's court: in the Middle Ages many citizens moved here to avoid the Corporation's restrictive tariffs.*

the street, and just beyond it on the left is the 12th-century church of **St John the Baptist (52)**. Because this area of Winchester fell on hard times, the church has happily been very little altered over the years, and its interior has the authentic feel of the Middle Ages, enhanced by the outline of 13th-century wall paintings on the north side. A little further up the hill on the left you will find a 14th-century timbered house, **Old Blue Boar House (54)**, said to be the oldest residence in Winchester.

Returning down St John's Street, turn right over the bridge, and you are entering the medieval city at the site of the former Eastgate. In the Broadway on the right is the medieval porch and chapel of **St John's Hospital (6)**. This charity may be as old as the 10th century; it was established here by the early 1200s. Unlike St Cross it welcomed inmates of both sexes, drawing a substantial income from the commercial properties it owned in the city. In the 18th century, like St Cross, it suffered a decline and the chapel became a school; but a new trust was set up in 1829, and the almshouses on either side of the Broadway date mainly from that period. The **Abbey Gardens** on the south side of the street were until the Reformation the site of one of Alfred's great foundations, Nunnaminster, or the nunnery of the Abbey of St Mary. Its memory is preserved in the name of Abbey House, a pleasant brick building reconstructed privately in 1751 and given a fancifully Gothick street front. In 1890 the Corporation bought Abbey House to serve as the Mayor's residence, for it stands conveniently beside the elaborate Gothic Revival Guildhall (1871–3). Hamo Thornycroft's bronze **statue of King Alfred (1**; erected 1901) dominates the scene, looking up the line of the High Street – the spine of Roman Winchester and of the present city.

Places of Interest near Winchester

A visit to Winchester is incomplete without some exploration of the beautiful surrounding countryside, ranging from the flatter trout-stream country in the east to the rolling chalk downland in the west. Scattered over it lie interesting villages and market towns, each with a fine church and a story to tell.

Routes in three directions suggest themselves: starting to the south-west and following the River Test north; following the River Itchen out to the north-east; and taking the old Pilgrims Way to the south-east.

North with the Test

Romsey (57) The great abbey was founded in 907 by Edward, son of Alfred the Great, for his daughter Elfleda, but it was sacked by the Danes and little remained of that period. Dating mainly from the years 1120–1250, what we see today gives one of the best impressions of a major Norman convent church to be found in England (it is 263 feet long, and 127 feet wide across the transepts).

Over the years, rumours of scandals involving the nuns were rife but little was substantiated, though one abbess was forced to resign after an official visitation in 1502. The townspeople were able to purchase the abbey after the Dissolution in 1539, so the church at least was saved from destruction. The famous Romsey Rood, a stone crucifix with the hand of God showing above the cross, on the outer west wall of the south transept, is probably early 11th century. Inside, the church's treasures include an even earlier crucifix – a Saxon one, carved in wood (east end of the south choir aisle).

Romsey is a compact, lively town. Of its many interesting buildings the oldest is 'King John's House' opposite the abbey, a 13th-century upper hall house. That infamous monarch's name was often given to ancient buildings of unknown origin and there may well be no real connection. Lord Palmerston's statue stands in the square and his home, Broadlands, is to the south of the town. More recently, the imposing house in its 400-acre estate belonged to Lord Mountbatten and saw numerous royal visits.

The River Test flows here, but to see it from the town go to the gardens off Mill Street where you can feed the trout.

Mottisfont (55) The simple aisleless church contains three surprises: the powerful Norman chancel arch, fine 15th-century glass in the east window, and an elaborate Elizabethan family monument. Mottisfont Abbey (56) is well worth visiting: converted into a house after the Dissolution, it incorporates the remains of an Augustinian priory founded in 1201. A little

55 Mottisfont church, looking east: the chancel arch is Norman, the chancel mainly 13th century. The east window's 15th-century glass shows the crucifixion, St Andrew (to whom the church is dedicated) and St Peter. Above are Christ and the Virgin, and at the very top, the crucified Christ in the lap of God.

upstream from here the river is particularly interesting and something remains of what was probably the earliest reservoir in the country.

King's Somborne Between the river and the village, numerous bridges cross a small stream and the 15th-century boundary banks of John of Gaunt's deer park can be seen. This is a pretty village with many thatched cottages built of traditional materials; the fine church contains good brasses and has been well restored.

Farley Mount Take a pleasant walk to the top of this bronze age barrow near the route of the Roman road between Salisbury and Winchester, to enjoy the beauty of the surrounding countryside and to read the monument to the horse which landed safely with its rider after a sheer drop of 25 feet: renamed 'Beware Chalk Pit', it went on to win several races.

Stockbridge The Grosvenor Hotel is the traditional venue for the fly fishermen of the River Test. This delightful river rises at Ashe, 20 miles upstream, amid a mass of water mint and marsh grasses; soon increasing in size, it divides and rejoins continually as it flows along its wide valley. Stop and stare into the racing waters and you will see the speckled brown trout

56 The 18th-century south front of Mottisfont Abbey from its expansive grounds, which are planted with splendid trees. Just to the left of this picture is the spring which may be the reason for the medieval priory's foundation here; its crystal clear water, rising at the rate of 200 gallons a minute, joins the River Test, which borders the immaculate lawn.

57 *One of the strange carvings on the Norman capitals of the chancel of Romsey Abbey: this one in the south aisle shows two seated men with a monster's head, and (at left) a king and an angel. Just to the east of this carving is one of the abbey's great treasures, a Saxon carving of the crucifixion.*

holding himself against the stream. Catching him is a much more expensive business.

The 13th-century chancel of the Old Church which was pulled down in 1863 remains as the town's oldest monument, standing in an old graveyard and sheltered by trees. The substantial street (it suggests more behind, but this is deceptive) contains two fine early-19th-century inns and the Town Hall of the same period, as well as earlier buildings. Marsh Court, 1 mile south, is by Sir Edwin Lutyens and has the rare distinction of being built entirely of chalk.

To the north-west stands Danebury Hill, a prehistoric camp with burial mounds going back to Neolithic times and with a history of subsequent human occupation. It has been partly excavated, and makes a good climb for the energetic.

The Itchen

Headbourne Worthy is the first of the four 'Worthies' encountered as you follow the Itchen north out of Winchester and is unfortunately close to the busy junction of the main A33 and A34 roads. The church is notable for the extent of its Saxon fabric and particularly for its Saxon stone rood (crucifix) on the tower's inner wall (compare Romsey).

Martyr Worthy For those with time to spare, the pleasantest way to reach the group of villages to the east of the busy roads which now include the M3 is to take the footpath from the city walls recreation ground, following the river. Martyr Worthy contains some sensitively restored timber-framed thatched cottages (**58**), and the village street slopes down attractively past the church (late Norman) to a footpath and bridge over the river leading to Easton, another charming village well worth a visit.

Itchen Abbas contains large houses set in pleasant gardens and is a convenient starting point for some beautiful river walks. Charles Kingsley

visited the village and fished in the river, which may have suggested some scenes in his book *The Water Babies*. A road crossing the river leads south to **Avington**. The fine 18th-century church at the edge of Avington Park – the chapel of the house – with a spendidly complete original interior of Spanish mahogany box pews and three-decker pulpit, should not be missed.

New Alresford (pronounced 'Allsford') is a planned town, established in 1200 at the time when the Itchen was made navigable from here to Southampton, both projects being initiated by the enterprising Bishop de Lucy of Winchester. Tree-lined Broad Street justifies its name and must be one of the best village streets in the county. The many 18th-century (and some earlier) houses here and in West and East Streets (**59**) are worth leisurely consideration – early on a Sunday morning, to avoid the usual heavy traffic and general bustle.

Tichborne (**60, 61**) The fascinating little church dates from the transitional period between Saxon and Norman building methods, and is complemented by a scattering of interestingly varied thatched cottages. As you pass, think of the two events involving the Tichborne family for which the village is widely known.

The first accounts for the annual Tichborne Dole: every Lady Day (25 March) a large measure of flour is given to householders during a quaint ceremony presided over by the priest. The right to the Dole (which was originally loaves of bread) was earned by a 12th-century wife of the Lord of the manor. On her deathbed she expressed concern for the poor, and was told that he would set aside as much land for their benefit as she could crawl around during the time it took a brand to burn. She managed to get around 20 acres before dying, and the land has been known as 'The Crawls' ever since. For good measure she laid a curse on the Tichborne family should the Dole ever be discontinued.

The second event is the notorious affair of the 'Tichborne Claimant'. In 1871 the heir to the manor was missing and generally assumed to be drowned. Only his mother was not convinced and advertised widely for him. A butcher from Wagga Wagga in Australia responded and was accepted by Lady Tichborne before she died, despite the fact that he was a 24-stone giant of a man and the long lost heir had been a slight little fellow. We can marvel equally at how well the claimant prepared himself with witnesses and background information, and at the efficiency of the English legal system at that time, when we learn that it took a trial lasting a hundred days for the Tichbornes to resist his claim and a further trial of 188 days to have him convicted of fraud and sentenced to 14 years imprisonment.

59 *The Old School House in West Street, New Alresford.*

The Old Pilgrims Way

Cheesefoot Head The A272 follows much of the course of the Pilgrims Way and is a delightful drive out of Winchester. Among the spectacular views is Cheesefoot Head, a great natural amphitheatre 3 miles east of Winchester. Imagine it packed with troops listening in different attitudes of concentration as Eisenhower addressed them before the 1944 D-Day landings. After dry weather the foundations of what was possibly a Roman building show through the grass.

The Meon Valley After about 10 miles turn south onto the A32. Unfortunately this busy road detracts from the many pleasant cottages in **West Meon**, but turn off it to see Garden Cottage, a good example of the older houses in the village. **Meonstoke** is by-passed by the main road. From the church beside the river the main street gently curves, providing examples of harmonious development over four centuries. Nearby Corhampton church is a late-Saxon building with a Saxon sundial on the south wall.

If you follow the river back to **East Meon**, where it runs down the middle of a particularly pretty High Street, you will find what Pevsner calls 'one of the most thrilling village churches in Hampshire', with a Norman tower

61 Tichborne church stands on land which belonged in Saxon times to Winchester's Oldminster, being given to the minster by King Cenwalh in the 7th century. The 11th-century chancel windows are of a kind known in only one other church (in Oxfordshire); the box pews and communion rail are Jacobean; and the tower, seen here, is dated 1703.

60 The superb alabaster monument (1621) of Sir Benjamin Tichborne, gentleman of the Privy Chamber to James I, and his wife Dame Amphillis, with their four sons and three daughters, in the north aisle of Tichborne church, which forms the Tichborne family chapel and is filled with Tichborne hatchments and memorials dating from the 16th century to the 20th. Sir Benjamin's tilting helm hangs over the entrance.

and a tremendous 12th-century black marble font (**62**), comparable with the one in Winchester Cathedral. The Court House east of the church (14th century) belonged to the bishops of Winchester.

Here you are near to three places with literary connections.

Steep The name aptly describes the sharply rising country 3 miles north of Petersfield. Follow a path opposite the church to the Edward Thomas memorial for magnificent views of the area. The poet and country writer had a favourite working den in a room in a house nearby. He was killed in

62 *East Meon church font, decorated for the church's flower festival. Made in Tournai from a single block of recrystallised limestone, it was brought here c. 1150 and may have been the gift of Henry de Blois, bishop of Winchester. The carvings tell the story of the Creation and Fall and the life of the spirit. Here composite interlaced creatures over pillars and arches represent the appearance of life on the earth; other sides portray the creation of Adam and Eve, their fall, their expulsion from Paradise (a Romanesque palace) and the angel showing Adam how to dig while Eve practises spinning. On the top doves peck grapes and drink wine – an ancient symbol of the eternal life of the Christian spirit.*

the Battle of Arras in 1918, when most of his poetry was still unpublished. **Selborne** is best known as the home of Gilbert White (1720–93), the clergyman whose remarkable observations of his surroundings made him a pioneer of natural history. *The Natural History and Antiquities of Selborne*, published when he was 70, still reads freshly today. He helped to create the zigzag path which climbs the steep 'Selborne Hanger', a beech-covered hill giving fine views of the village. His house, The Wakes, is now a museum to himself and Captain Oates (1880–1912), the Antarctic explorer who perished with Scott.

Chawton The little red house at the meeting of the roads was Jane Austen's home from 1809 until the last year of her life. Here she wrote *Mansfield Park*, *Emma* and *Persuasion*, working in the family sitting-room and hiding her manuscript under the blotter when anyone approached through the helpfully creaking door. During these seven years all her novels except *Northanger Abbey* were published. She left Chawton to seek medical advice at Winchester, where she died (see pp. 50–2). The house is now a museum to her. Half a mile south is Chawton House, home of her brother Edward.

APPROACHES TO THE CENTRE

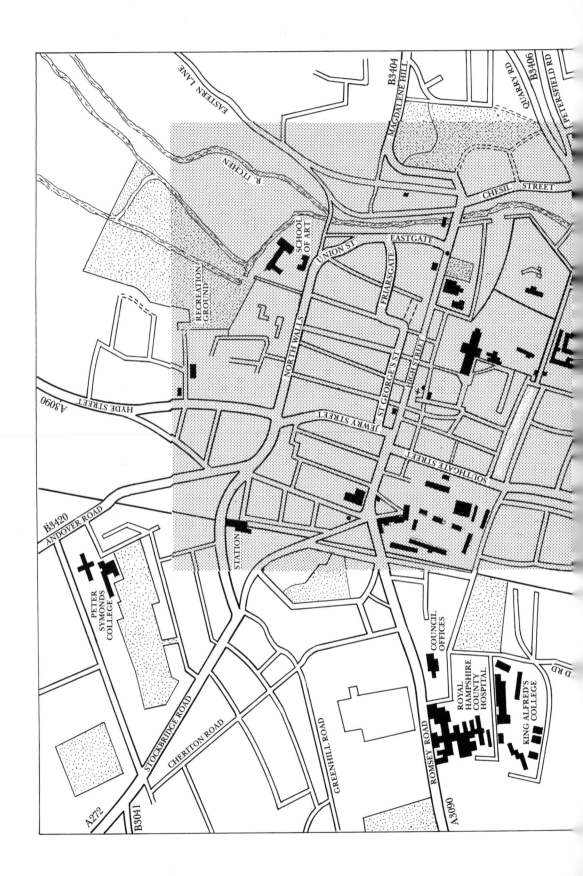

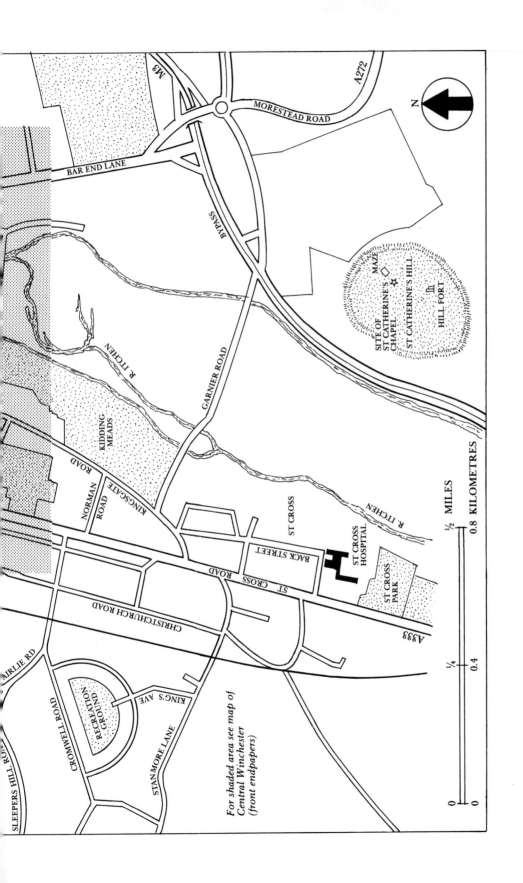